Christopher Lascelles was born in London in 1971 and studied modern languages and history at St Andrews University in Scotland. He is the author of *Pontifex Maximus: A Short History of the Popes.*

A SHORT HISTORY OF THE WORLD

CHRISTOPHER LASCELLES

History, n. an account, mostly false, of events, mostly unimportant, which are brought about by rulers, mostly knaves, and soldiers, mostly fools.

AMBROSE BIERCE, *The Devil's Dictionary*

'To be ignorant of what happened before you were born is to be ever a child.'

MARCUS TULLIUS CICERO, *Roman Orator*

'Who controls the past controls the future; who controls the present controls the past.'

GEORGE ORWELL, *Author*

'It is difficult at times to repress the thought that history is about as instructive as an abattoir.'

SEAMUS HEANEY, *Poet*

Contents

List of Maps

Maps produced by ML Design

Preface

History is generally taught in an episodic, fragmentary fashion, leaving students with a lifelong lack of understanding as to how each part relates to the whole. We learn about the Fire of London, Christopher Columbus and the Second World War, but we are seldom given a coherent picture of how they all fit together.

As a young boy, I remember making an active decision to stop studying history, put off as I was by bad teaching and the proliferation of dates that I could never hope to remember. I was equally frustrated that I could not visualise where all the places were; Napoleon may well have been defeated at Waterloo, but where on earth was Waterloo?

Those who wish they had a better general knowledge of world history often find themselves time-poor and caught up in information overload. The result is that not everyone has the time, or the focus, to read a long history book.

This book is a response to all these problems. It aims to give a short (actually, very short – I attempted initially to write it in 100 pages) and succinct yet broad overview of the key developments and events in the history of mankind in a way that is, I hope, enlightening and interesting.

I do not profess to add any new insight or to unearth any new information; there are plenty of historians much better qualified to do that than I. I aim only to condense the generally accepted mainstream view into a simplified linear whole. While each country, each key character, each movement and each discovery deserves its own book – if not its own library – I have purposefully kept this book as brief as possible in order to make the information accessible to the widest range of people.

I hope that you enjoy it and that it fills the gaps.

Christopher Lascelles
London, April 2019

I

PRE-HISTORY

(The Big Bang – 3500 BC)

The Beginning

There is a consensus among members of the scientific community that the universe in which we live burst into existence following a cataclysmic explosion, or 'Big Bang', 13.7 billion years ago. The swirling masses of matter and energy that resulted from this Big Bang were pulled together by electrostatic forces over the coming billions of years to form galaxies, stars and planets, including the one on which we live.

Earth is a small planet in a galaxy we call the Milky Way, whose total number of stars is unknown, although estimates range from 100 billion to 400 billion. What's more, there are supposedly at least 100 billion other galaxies in the known universe. That is a lot of stars and an incredible amount of space, if you consider that the average distance between two stars is roughly 30 trillion miles.

About 4.5 billion years ago, gaseous, solid and other matter pulled together to form Earth. A few hundred million years later, it is thought that a huge object, or maybe even another planet, crashed into Earth, blowing out enough matter to form a satellite body, which then became our moon. After this literally earth-shattering event, Earth took millions of years to cool down.

A bombardment of meteors may have brought water to Earth in the form of ice. As the planet's crust cooled, water vapour emissions from volcanoes condensed and accumulated as oceans after rain from the newly formed atmosphere no longer evaporated on the planet's hot surface.

Life

Approximately 3.5 billion years ago, when the land was still a hostile place dominated by volcanoes, microscopic single-celled organisms made of complex organic molecules appeared deep in these new oceans. These organisms were the most advanced life-forms on the planet for another 3 billion years, until suddenly (relatively speaking that is), within the period of a few million years, bacteria in the sea began processing carbon dioxide, water and sunlight to produce oxygen. This helped some of the single-celled organisms to begin joining together in colonies, eventually creating multi-cellular organisms.

Through reproduction, these primitive creatures began to evolve, and eventually, when there was enough oxygen in the atmosphere to protect against the sun's radiation, some emerged from the sea. As life evolved and adapted to occupy the many different niches in the earth's ecosystems over the next few hundred million years, the diversity of organisms expanded from these common ancestors to what exists today: insects, amphibians, reptiles, birds and mammals. Only religious fundamentalists (creationists) dispute this generally accepted explanation. Remarkably, there is a large number of people who still believe that our planet is only 6,000 years old.

During this process, there will have been countless intermediate forms (missing links) and evolutionary dead-ends, most of which we will never know, as geologists recognise at least five episodes in the history of our planet when life was destroyed, suddenly and extensively, in mass extinctions. We don't know for certain what caused all these extinctions, although suggestions have ranged from meteor impacts to solar flares and volcanic upheavals, all of which could have caused sudden global warming or cooling, changing sea levels, or epidemics.

The two largest of these were the Permian Mass Extinction and the K-T Extinction.[1] The Permian Mass Extinction of 250 million years ago wiped out up to 96 percent of species existing at the time due to a drastic decline in oxygen levels. The K-T Extinction of 65 million years ago destroyed the dinosaurs that had already roamed our planet for close to 150 million years.

This puts the six or seven thousand years since the appearance of the first proper human civilisations into perspective. Given the length of time in which we have existed in relation to the beginning of our planet, it is not unimaginable that human life could also become extinct – and perhaps a lot sooner than we think – for any number of reasons, including those above.

The Birth of Man and the Exploration of the Earth

From the very little evidence we have,[2] it is generally understood that ape-like primates first appeared in the forests of Eastern Africa roughly 20–30 million years ago. We don't know exactly when bipedalism (walking on two feet) evolved. A long-held theory was that climate change destroyed the

---

[1]   K-T signifies Cretaceous-Tertiary, which are both names of geological periods.

[2]   The little evidence we have for the evolution of man revolves around a very small number of skull and skeletal fragments found in different parts of the world and theories are constantly being revised.

primates' natural habitat, forcing them out into the open savannah, where they evolved the ability to stand in order to keep an eye out for predators, but evolutionary biologists now believe that bipedalism had already developed during the tree-dwelling phase. Either way, walking on two legs helped free the hands of our distant ancestors and enabled them to carry food and children. This meant that it was much easier to travel longer distances and explore the world.

Another huge evolutionary advantage came with the ability to use tools. 2.5 million years ago a species of these hominins (early humans) began using tools, as evidenced by materials found with their remains. As a result, the species was named *Homo habilis* or 'Handy Man', and is generally thought to be the first direct ancestor of *Homo sapiens*, or modern humans. Other classifications such as *Homo ergaster*, *Homo erectus*, *Homo heidelbergensis* and the better-known *Homo neanderthalensis*, or 'Neanderthal Man', have been variously assigned to the fossils of our early relatives who are believed to have lived between *Homo habilis* and the present day, with each one evolving greater brain capacity over time.

The fossil record suggests that by a million years ago *Homo erectus* ('Upright Man'), our first ancestor to walk truly upright, had spread across the world, having migrated outwards from East Africa.[3] There then follow two schools of thought: one is the Multi-Regional Theory of Evolution, which states that humans thereafter evolved separately wherever they made their home. The other, more generally accepted view is that there was a second major migratory movement[4] by *Homo sapiens* (Wise Man) once again out of

---

[3]   This is called the 'Out of Africa' theory.

[4]   In all likelihood, there were other migrations between the two.

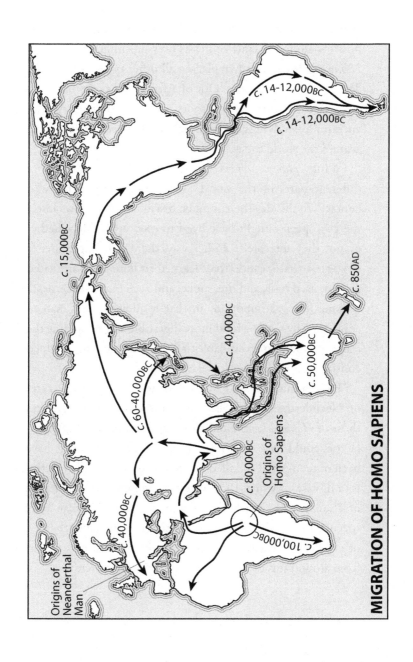

MIGRATION OF HOMO SAPIENS

Origins of Neanderthal Man

Origins of Homo Sapiens

c. 15,000BC

c. 14-12,000BC

c. 14-12,000BC

c. 850AD

c. 40,000BC

c. 50,000BC

c. 60-40,000BC

c. 40,000BC

c. 80,000BC

c. 100,000BC

Africa, starting approximately 60-80,000 years ago – very possibly along the same routes as previous migrations – with *Homo sapiens* gradually replacing all other types of hominid. The assumptions for the 'Out of Africa' theory are based on research that has traced our roots back to a common African ancestor by studying genetic differences between people living around the world today.

While *Homo sapiens* and Neanderthals originated in different parts of the world,[5] they nevertheless came into contact. To this day there is much discussion as to how closely the two species might have lived to each other and whether or not they interbred.[6] Either way, there is strong evidence to suggest that Neanderthals learned to hunt in coordinated groups, used tools and fire, spoke, and even buried their dead. Making fire was important in that it allowed early man to cook, thereby making food more digestible and expanding the range of food sources available to him. This would have helped considerably with man's social evolution.

From around 30,000 BC – with few exceptions – traces of Neanderthals (and all other hominids) disappear, and those of *Homo sapiens* rapidly increase. A number of different factors could have been responsible: Neanderthals may have been outcompeted or killed by *Homo sapiens*, or fallen victim to a disease to which they were not immune or to a change of climate with which they could not cope. We can only speculate about these, or a host of other reasons, given the lack of conclusive evidence. What we do know, however, is that from around this time, *Homo sapiens* reigned supreme.

---

[5]   Neanderthals originated in Europe while *Homo sapiens* originated in Africa.

[6]   We share 99.5 per cent of our DNA with Neanderthals.

We do not currently know if the causes for human migrations were competition for resources, climate change or simply the desire to explore. Regardless of the reasons, the general view is that Australia was colonised approximately 50,000 years ago and that, by circa 15,000 BC, *Homo sapiens* had crossed into present-day Alaska via what is now the Bering Strait, when it was either dry land or frozen water. Then, within a few thousand years, they reached the southernmost tip of South America and, with the exception of a few islands in the Pacific, had colonised most of the world.[7] From then on, life in the Americas would develop in complete isolation from the rest of the world until European colonisation began in 1492, notwithstanding a brief visit by the Vikings around AD 1000.

From Hunter-gathering to Farming

Humans initially led a nomadic 'hunter-gatherer' existence, moving from area to area, hunting animals and eating any digestible foods they could find, such as plants, nuts, berries and fruit. Eventually, people began returning every year to the most fertile places. About 10,000 years ago, it seems humans worked out how to sow crops – a discovery that allowed them to move from hunting and gathering to farming. This had such a significant effect on the subsequent development of mankind that it has been named the 'Neolithic Revolution.'[8]

Once people began living near each other, increased communications led to greater co-operation and to the exchange of knowledge. Yet it was the availability of more

---

[7] Earth's history has been characterised by the coming and going of long ice ages. The Bering Strait may have been frozen just before the end of the last ice age in around 12,000 BC, allowing man to make the journey between the two continents.

[8] Neolithic means 'New Stone Age'.

food that was fundamental to how mankind developed: plentiful food led to expanding populations, which in turn led to more settlements. The ability to produce and store food also meant that societies were eventually able to support non-food-producing specialists such as artisans, holy men, bureaucrats and soldiers as well as political leaders.

Whilst yarn for clothing could be produced from the fibres of certain crops, other sources of clothing were provided by the wool and hides of animals such as sheep, goats, cows and pigs, all of which mankind gradually domesticated. These animals also helped in other ways: their manure increased crop yields, whilst their labour – pulling ploughs – made more land suitable for farming.

A productive virtuous circle was thus established. However living together in permanent dwellings came with a downside: humans were now dwelling near their own refuse and excrement at a time when they neither understood the benefits of cleanliness nor knew about the existence of germs. Living in closer quarters with livestock also meant that diseases, which had developed in animals and to which humans had no immunity, were now able to cross the species barrier. The major killers of humanity through the centuries – smallpox, flu, tuberculosis, malaria, measles, plague, cholera and AIDS – are all thought to have evolved originally in animals, transferring to humans via fleas or other carriers.

Nor was this process confined to pre-history: plagues and influenza throughout history may all have originated in this way. The 21st century is no exception, with Swine Flu and Bird Flu acting as nasty reminders that intensive rearing of animals, with all its ethically dubious practices, might still come back to bite us.

II

THE ANCIENT WORLD

(3500 BC – AD 500)

The First Civilisations

The earliest evidence of complex societies that we have (and this may change with future excavations) dates from around 3500 BC, and comes from Mesopotamia – modern-day Iraq and Syria. The mild wet winters and long, dry, hot summers characteristic of the area were ideal for growing crops, and it is here, as far as we know, that plants were first domesticated. Importantly, the land was also located between two major rivers – the Tigris and the Euphrates – which provided ready access to water and thus to irrigation.[9] When viewed on a map, the area itself is crescent-shaped, and for this reason, along with that of the fertility of its land, it has been named the 'Fertile Crescent'.

Mesopotamia was at the crossroads of Africa, Europe and Asia – a convenient location for people to meet to trade goods and share ideas. The area had few natural boundaries, however, and was therefore difficult to defend. As a result, its history for many millenia is that of rising and falling kingdoms and continuous territorial wars. Given the numerous shifts in power over this period, and a general lack of historical source material, it is not always easy to follow.

---

[9]   The word 'Mesopotamia' comes from the Greek 'mesos'- middle, and 'potamos' – river, i.e. land between the rivers.

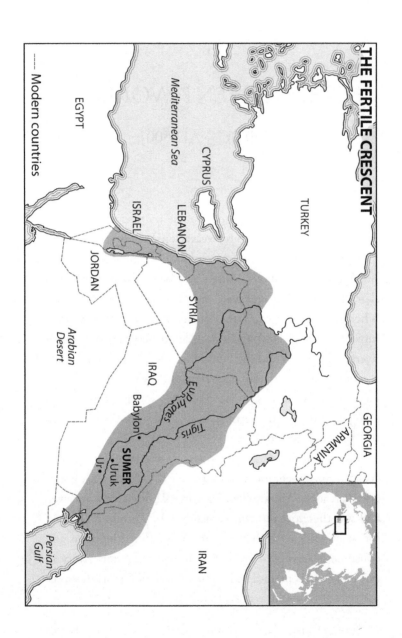

THE FERTILE CRESCENT

— Modern countries

EGYPT

Mediterranean Sea

CYPRUS

TURKEY

ISRAEL

LEBANON

JORDAN

SYRIA

ARMENIA

GEORGIA

Arabian
Desert

IRAQ

Euphrates

Tigris

Babylon

SUMER

Uruk

Ur

Persian
Gulf

IRAN

One of the earliest civilisations in the world – that of Sumer – dominated southern Mesopotamia from approximately 3300 to 2000 BC. It is generally believed that the Sumerians were the first people to establish cities of up to 50,000 inhabitants. Sumer's main city of Uruk may well have been the largest in the world at one time, and some temples from this period still stand in Iraq today, although sadly, Islamic fundamentalists have done their best to destroy them. Sumerian civilisation also provides the earliest example of one of the most important developments for humankind: writing in the form of pictograms used by temple officials to record basic information about crops and taxes. Apart from what we have surmised about world history through archaeology and geology, there is very little actual detail until the appearance of writing, and its emergence acts as the dividing line between pre-history and history.

Ancient Egypt: Land of the Pharaohs (3100 BC)

Around the same time, another civilisation sprang up in Egypt along the banks of the Nile – a river whose annual floods provided the much-needed water for irrigating crops. The fertility of the soil around the Nile contributed significantly to the growth of Egyptian wealth and power, as Egypt became an exporter of food to other parts of the Mediterranean and the Middle East. Moreover, the desert acted as a defensive barrier to would-be invaders, thus ensuring political stability in the land.

In circa 3100 BC, this patchwork of different kingdoms was united under a powerful king, or pharaoh, called Nemes. He built the capital, Memphis, from which Egyptian dynasties ruled for the next thousand years. Egypt became the largest kingdom in the world, with up to a million subjects ruled by approximately 30 different dynasties over the following 2,500 years. The pharaohs were recognised as gods by the population.

Funerary practices – those dealing with death and burial – were particularly important in Egyptian religion, which partly explains the dedication with which the pharaohs built the great pyramids – in effect giant tombstones – between 2700 and 2200 BC. Incredibly, even today, nobody really knows exactly how they were constructed, and their height was unsurpassed for millennia. Indeed, the Great Pyramid of Khufu at Giza, built over 4,500 years ago, was the tallest building on Earth for over 3,000 years, until Lincoln Cathedral, completed in England in AD 1311, stole that title. It was only a short-lived honour, however, as its record-breaking wooden spire collapsed a mere 250 years later.

Civilisations in the East

Beyond Egypt and Mesopotamia, two other major independent civilisations arose along other waterways – one in north-west India along the Indus River, crossing into present-day Pakistan and Afghanistan, and the other along the Yellow River in China.

Founded around the turn of the third millennium, the Indus Valley Civilisation – often referred to at its peak as the Harappan Civilisation, after its major city of Harappa – covered a huge area of land almost the size of western Europe. Although a number of unanswered questions remain about this society, partly due to the fact that its writing has still not been deciphered, we do know that Harappa and its sister city, Mohenjo-Daro, were major conurbations, supporting populations of over 30,000 people and trading with each other as well as with Mesopotamia. Their people were clearly advanced, as they lived in brick and stone houses, cultivated

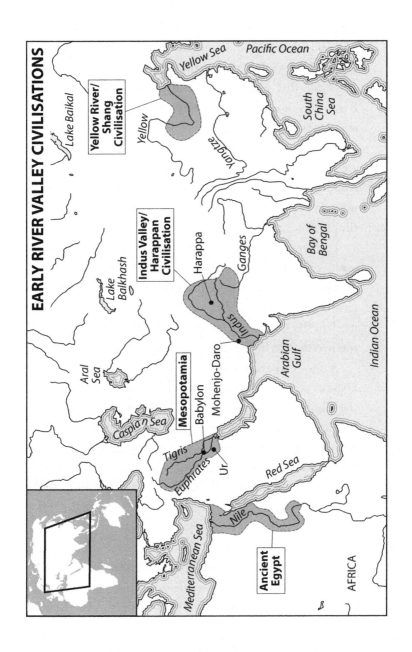

wheat and barley and irrigated fields. Moreover, both cities were laid out in grids and similarly constructed, thus suggesting a unified, or at least collaborative, government.

While this society flourished between 2600 and 2000 BC, its major cities were suddenly abandoned between 1700 and 1600 BC, with the entire society ceasing to exist by around 1300 BC. Although the exact causes of this decline are unknown, suggestions include climate change; erosion and degradation of the soil that prompted the population to migrate eastwards; and invasion by Indo-Europeans[10] from the north-west.

Further east, the earliest empire for which we have written evidence is the Shang Dynasty, which established a kingdom along the banks of the Yellow River around 1700 BC. Its territory covered an area of approximately one tenth of modern-day China, and it lasted for roughly 700 years, until it was overthrown by the Chou (or Zhou) Dynasty.

A few barbarian invasions notwithstanding, the Chou Dynasty was of a similar duration. Yet for most of this time, the Chou were merely the most powerful rulers among the hundred or more quasi-independent principalities in the region. Interestingly, unlike the Harappan Civilisation in India that suddenly disappeared, the beliefs and system of government of these early Chinese dynasties formed the foundations on which subsequent ones would rule the region until well into the 20th century.

The Hittites: Early Ironmongers (1400–1200 BC)

Back in western Asia another major empire surfaced in the second millennium BC – that of the Hittites. By the mid-

---

[10]   Indo-Europeans were a people who originated in an area between the Black Sea and the Caspian Sea.

14th century BC they had carved out an empire comprising present-day Turkey and parts of present-day Lebanon and Iraq. It was the Hittites who discovered how to smelt iron ore to make iron. This was recognised as an extremely important development, as armies possessing more resilient iron weapons could vanquish those that were poorly armed with bronze. Although the Hittites sold iron tools to other countries, they opted not to share knowledge of how to make them, and it was this that made them the chief power in the area for some 200 years.

The Olmecs of Central America (1400–400 BC)

Over on the other side of the world, another distinct civilisation developed in Central America: that of the Olmecs. We know less about the Olmecs than about their major Asian counterparts, as they left very few written records, and few traces can be found that date after 400 BC for reasons unknown (although it was very possibly due to environmental change). We know that they had a calendar, carved gigantic stone heads, built large pyramid-like structures and traded extensively. Their religious life included bloodletting and human sacrifice, and their rituals and beliefs formed the basis of those of the civilisations that would inhabit the area after them, including the Mayans and the Aztecs.

The Invasion of the Sea Peoples (1200 BC)

A turning point in the history of the old Mediterranean world came around 1200 BC, when a confederacy of predominantly seafaring raiders from the north and the west emigrated eastwards. Egyptian texts refer to them as the 'Sea Peoples'.

The Stone, Bronze & Iron Ages

Before 5000 BC, tools and weapons were predominantly made from stone, wood and bone, hence the term 'Stone Age'. When humans discovered that metals could be extracted from ore at high temperatures, copper began to be used for tools, albeit to a limited degree.[11] However, sometime around 3300 BC, it was discovered that heating a mixture of copper and tin ore at the ratio of 9:1 could produce an even more durable material – bronze. Thus began what we now refer to as the 'Bronze Age'.

The different ages did not begin or end everywhere simultaneously: the British Isles, for example, only entered the Bronze Age in around 800 BC, and even into the 20th century several Stone Age civilisations were still being discovered.

Iron began to be used in significant quantities in the Middle East and south-east Europe around the 13th century BC, shortly after people discovered how to produce the necessary heat to smelt iron ore from rock. Much stronger and more ubiquitous than copper and tin, iron gradually overtook bronze as the most sought-after metal. As with the Bronze Age, the Iron Age began at different times across the world, only reaching northern Europe in around 600 BC.

The northern group of invaders settled on the coast of present-day Lebanon – an area that the Greeks later referred to as 'Phoenicia'. The southern group of invaders, the Peleste – subsequently known as the Philistines – was prevented from entering Egypt, and ended up in Canaan – an area corresponding roughly to modern-day Israel, Palestine, Lebanon and southern Syria. Like other peoples in the region, the Philistines were ultimately unable to withstand pressure

---

[11]   In all likelihood, the Egyptians built their early pyramids with only copper and stone utensils, which makes the pyramids an even greater achievement than we might at first think, notwithstanding the untold misery of the workers that the process must have entailed.

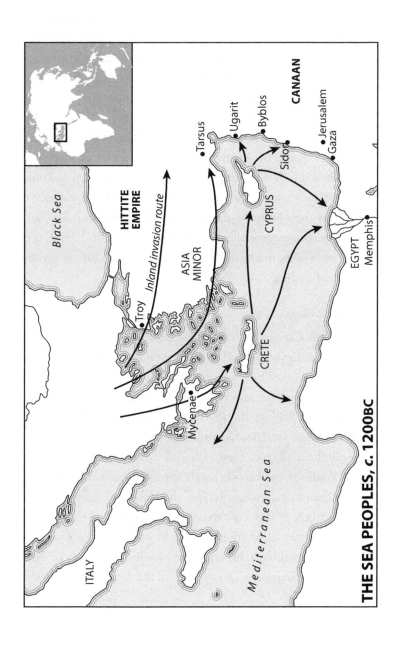

THE SEA PEOPLES, c. 1200BC

Black Sea

HITTITE
EMPIRE

Inland invasion route

Troy

ASIA
MINOR

Tarsus

Ugarit

Byblos

Sidon

CANAAN

Jerusalem

Gaza

CYPRUS

EGYPT

Memphis

CRETE

Mycenae

Mediterranean Sea

ITALY

from the great powers around them, and disappeared from history in the 7th century BC, leaving only their name, Philistia (or Palestine), to designate the territory they had occupied.

Today it remains unclear who the Sea Peoples were, where they originated from[12] or even why they came. They may have migrated due to dramatic climate change, earthquakes or famine, or may have been pushed out by invading northern tribes. Equally, they may simply have been one of successive waves of invaders looking for land to farm. What we do know is that they wreaked havoc and destruction all the way down the east coast of the Mediterranean, and that following violent conquests they generally burnt cities to the ground. From this time onwards, the history of ancient Egypt is also marked by gradual decline.

The Hebrews

It was in Canaan that the Hebrews, having recently escaped slavery in Egypt, looked to build their own kingdom. Under attack from the Philistines the Hebrews put aside their quarrels with one another, and at some point in the 10th century BC appointed Saul as the first king of their territory – Israel. The biblical stories of Samson, Samuel, Saul, and David and Goliath are all concerned with Philistine-Hebrew conflicts.

Finding themselves in a state of permanent war, and fearing that their culture might be lost, the Hebrews began to record their history, and continued to do so over the following centuries in writings that came to be known as the Tanakh – the Hebrew Bible. Christians and Muslims base many of their religious beliefs on what is written in the Tanakh. It is also the

---

[12]   Greece, Crete and even Italy have all been suggested as their place of origin.

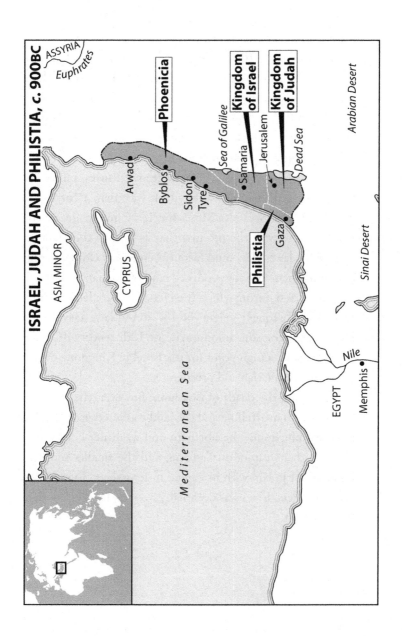

ISRAEL, JUDAH AND PHILISTIA, c. 900BC

textual source, with a few alterations in the order of books, for the Christian Old Testament.

We read in the Torah – the first five books of the Tanakh – that Abraham and his people had been driven out of southern Mesopotamia by invading tribes a thousand years previously (some 4,000 years ago). At some point, possibly to escape a famine, they had taken refuge in Egypt, only to be enslaved by the Egyptians. Sometime in the 1200s BC, as recalled in the book of Exodus, the Hebrew leader, Moses, rallied his people and led them out of Egypt. It was then, according to the Torah, that God gave Moses the Ten Commandments on Mount Sinai, with the promise that as long as the Hebrews obeyed his laws, He would favour them as his chosen people and bring them into the promised land of Canaan.

The period during which the Hebrews were led by Saul,[13] and the subsequent reigns of his son-in-law, David, and David's youngest son, Solomon, in the 10th century BC were, so we are told, a high point for the Israelite Kingdom, during which it became rich and prosperous.

Following the death of Solomon, however, the Hebrews fell back into quarrelling and the land was once again divided into two kingdoms: the northern and wealthier kingdom of Israel, with its capital in Samaria, and the smaller southern kingdom of Judah, with its capital in Jerusalem. Too weak to resist invaders, Israel was eventually overrun by the Assyrians from the east.

---

[13]   As related in the biblical Book of Samuel.

The Phoenicians Explore the Mediterranean (1000–500 BC)

The eastern Mediterranean area was not very rich in metals, which meant that the local inhabitants were forced to move westwards in search of new supplies. Between the turn of the millennium and 500 BC, the Phoenicians – descendants of the northern group of Sea Peoples who had settled in present-day Lebanon – and the sea-faring Greeks established settlements at strategic points along trade routes throughout the Mediterranean. One of the Phoenician settlements, Carthage, would ultimately play an important role in Roman history.

The Great Assyrian Empire

As the Sumerian civilisation in Mesopotamia slowly died around the turn of the second millennium BC, the kingdoms of Babylonia and Assyria, together with a number of tribes from present-day Iran and the Hittites from present-day Turkey, battled for supremacy. The kingdom of Babylonia, under various guises, generally predominated for much of the second millennium BC, until power moved to the Assyrians in around 910 BC. From this point until around 625 BC, the Assyrian Empire, with an army renowned for efficient ruthlessness, became the strongest and greatest empire in south-west Asia.

Waging a war of conquest, the Assyrians defeated the Babylonians, destroyed Israel and the Phoenician cities and attacked Egypt. However, like all over-extended empires, their luck finally ran out. A dynastic squabble around 630 BC opened the empire to attack by a tribe called the Medes (from present-day Iran) in the east, who were aided by other tribes from the north and the south. Between them they succeeded

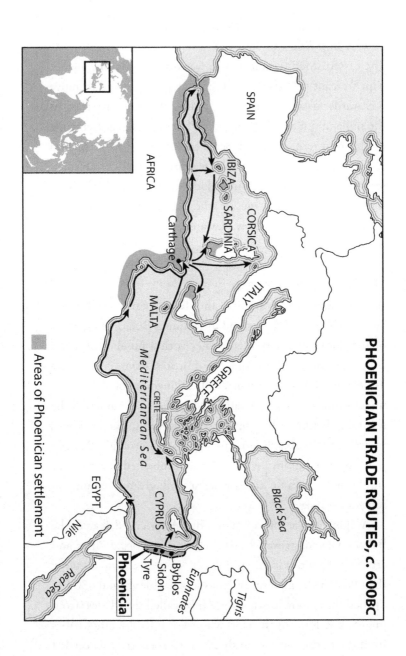

PHOENICIAN TRADE ROUTES, c. 600BC

■ Areas of Phoenician settlement

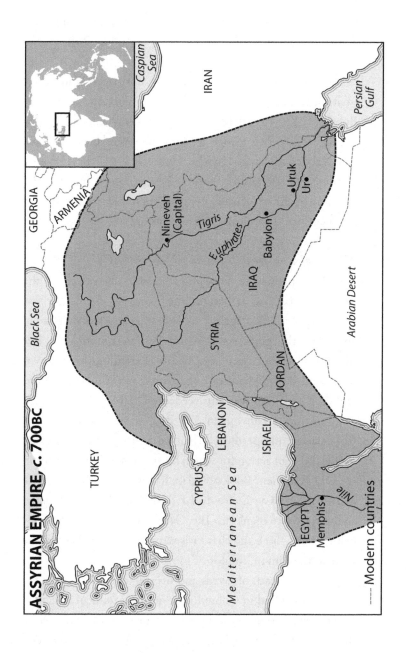

ASSYRIAN EMPIRE, c. 700BC

GEORGIA

ARMENIA

Caspian Sea

IRAN

Black Sea

TURKEY

Nineveh (Capital)

Tigris

Euphrates

Uruk

Ur

Babylon

IRAQ

Persian Gulf

CYPRUS

LEBANON

SYRIA

JORDAN

Arabian Desert

Mediterranean Sea

ISRAEL

EGYPT

Memphis

Nile

----- Modern countries

in conquering much of the Assyrian Empire, completely defeating it in 605 BC and burning its capital, Nineveh, to the ground.

During this war Jerusalem was destroyed and many of its inhabitants were taken into captivity in the city of Babylon. Yet the Babylonian civilisation managed only a brief resurgence under its king, Nabopolassar, and his son Nebuchadnezzar II (who famously built the Hanging Gardens of Babylon), before being conquered by the Persians in the 6th century BC and then, like so many of its predecessors, disappearing from history.

The Empire of Ancient Persia (550–330 BC)

The Parsa people, or Persians, were initially vassals of the Medes until Cyrus II became their king in 559 BC. It was Cyrus who rebelled against the Medes, captured their king, and built the great Achaemenid Persian Empire, the like of which had not been seen before. Extending from Egypt to present-day Afghanistan, the empire was built at a speed and on a scale that was unprecedented. When Cyrus and his army occupied Babylon in 539 BC, he freed the Hebrews from slavery and permitted them to return to their ancestral homeland – an action for which he was hailed as a liberator in the Old Testament Book of Isaiah. Known for his benevolence and tolerance, Cyrus also declared the first charter of human rights known to mankind. The 'Cyrus Cylinder' – a baked clay cylinder on which the charter is written – is now kept in the British Museum in London.

After the death of Cyrus and his son, the resulting power vacuum was filled in a bloodless coup by a nobleman named Darius, who claimed descent from an ancestor of Cyrus. With due modesty, he named himself 'King of Kings' and founded

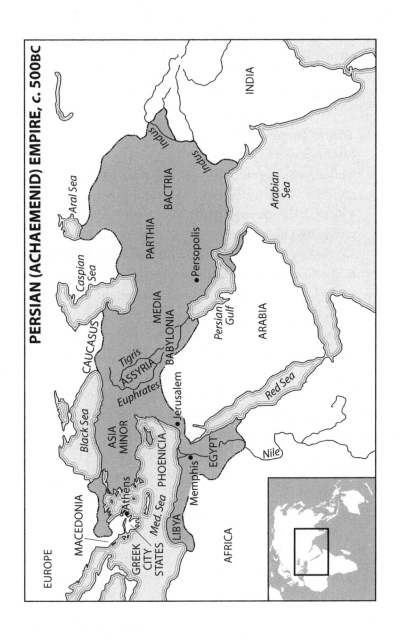

PERSIAN (ACHAEMENID) EMPIRE, c. 500BC

the city of Persepolis, which became the Persian capital. His campaigns, and those of his son Xerxes, which sought to bring the rebellious Greeks into submission, are some of the most written-about episodes of the period and lead us into the history of Ancient Greece.

Ancient Greece and the Greek City States (1000–330 BC)

Nothing which could properly be called a history book existed until the Greek historian Herodotus wrote one in around 450 BC. This means that we know very little about early Greece or, indeed, much of the ancient world. *The Iliad* and *The Odyssey* – epic poems from the 9th century BC attributed to the Greek poet Homer – provide us with much of what we do know about early Greece. However, the intertwining of myth and legend in these texts, along with scant archaeological evidence to back up their narrative, make them highly dubious as historical sources. *The Iliad* tells of the Mycenaean[14] attack on Troy (in today's west Turkey) led by Agamemnon. *The Odyssey* describes the ten-year journey home of the hero Odysseus – or Ulysses in Latin – after the fall of Troy, and includes the story of how he helped the Greeks to victory over the Trojans by sneaking a small army into the city in the belly of a wooden horse. Despite their doubtful historicity, however, they remain two of the most celebrated and widely read stories ever told.

We do know that the 8th century BC was generally an era of peace and prosperity for the Greeks. In their search for arable land – a search driven by living in a mountainous peninsula surrounded by islands – they created settlements on all the

---

[14] Mycenae was an early civilisation in present-day Greece which disappeared around the time of the Sea Peoples in circa 1200 BC.

islands in the Aegean Sea, and along the coasts of Asia Minor (present-day Turkey) and the Black Sea.

At this time Greece was not unified, but divided into populations of Aeolian, Dorian and Ionian Greeks. Small, fiercely patriotic city-states such as Athens were the norm. Generally trading with each other, but often at war, they only truly came together for defensive purposes against non-Greeks, whom they referred to as 'barbarians' due to the unintelligible 'bar-bar' sounds they supposedly made when speaking.

Beginning in 776 BC, the Greeks also came together every four years to compete in games held at Olympia in south-west Greece, during which all hostilities were suspended.[15] Athens grew to such an extent through trade and alliance that by 500 BC it had become the cultural, political and economic centre of Ancient Greece, and was recognised as such by other city-states.

In around 500 BC the Ionian Greeks, located on the shores of present-day Turkey, rebelled against Persian attempts to govern them. Frustrated by Athenian support for the Ionians, the Persians invaded, landing on the plains of Marathon, just north of Athens. The Athenians sent a trained runner to Sparta – a city-state renowned for the strength and valour of its soldiers, some 150 miles away – to request assistance. The Spartans agreed to assist, but only arrived after the battle was over. Nevertheless, the Ionian Greeks eventually managed to defeat Darius's numerically superior Persian army in 490 BC, and it was forced to return to Asia Minor. According to legend, an Athenian messenger was sent from Marathon to Athens, some 25 miles (40 km) away, where he announced the Persian defeat before dying of exhaustion. Since this time,

---

[15] The Olympic Games.

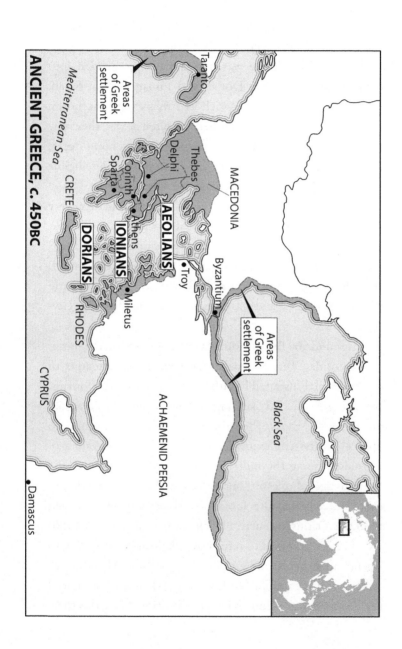

ANCIENT GREECE, c. 450BC

Areas of Greek settlement

Mediterranean Sea

Taranto

Delphi

Thebes

MACEDONIA

Corinth

Sparta

Athens

AEOLIANS

IONIANS

DORIANS

CRETE

RHODES

Troy

Byzantium

Miletus

Areas of Greek settlement

CYPRUS

Black Sea

ACHAEMENID PERSIA

Damascus

'marathon' has entered the English language as a long and arduous undertaking, including a long run.

Darius died before he could launch another invasion, but his defeat was not forgotten by the Persians. Ten years later, his son Xerxes led a second invasion of Greece in an attempt to avenge the losses at Marathon. This time the Persians reached a narrow pass at the valley of Thermopylae on the eastern coast of Greece. Legend has it that they were held off here by three hundred Spartans, led by their king, Leonidas, and only the help of a Greek traitor allowed them to find a way through.

Encouraged by their success, the Persians entered and destroyed Athens, whose population fled to the neighbouring island of Salamis. Despite possessing a vastly superior navy, the Persians were overcome at the sea battle of Salamis – history's first great naval conflict – and they never threatened Greece again.

Xerxes was eventually murdered, as was Darius III, the last of the Persian Achaemenids, in 330 BC. But the Greek victory was important for another reason: ultimately it was Greek rather than Persian culture that was bequeathed to the wider world, with Greek, along with Latin, gradually becoming the language of the educated classes throughout the Mediterranean.

With the Persians no longer a threat, Greece entered its classical period and witnessed a blossoming of culture, architecture and philosophy, during which the Greeks questioned the world around them. This search for knowledge resulted in Ancient Greece becoming known as the birthplace of philosophy and democracy. Philosophy comes from the Greek words *philo* and *sophia*, meaning 'love' and 'wisdom';

democracy comes from *demos* and *kratia* meaning 'people' and 'rule'.

Some of the most famous philosophers in history lived at this time: Socrates, who was sentenced to death for not believing in the state's gods and for corrupting the youth; his student, Plato, from whose writing we learn about Socrates, and who founded the first school of learning which he named the Academy; and Aristotle, the Academy's most famous student. Aristotle's father was the personal physician to Philip of Macedonia, and Aristotle himself was, for a time at least, the personal tutor of Alexander the Great, lecturing him on astronomy, physics, logic, politics, ethics, music, drama, poetry and a range of other subjects.

Keen to avenge themselves and prevent further Persian incursions into Greek territory, the Athenians persuaded a number of other Greek city-states to form a Naval League. This crumbled over the next twenty years, however, as the various cities were unable to refrain from their historic infighting. While these wars predominantly took place between the Spartans and the Athenians, they nevertheless took their toll on the entire area, including Persia, which had aided the Spartans.

The king of neighbouring Macedon, Philip II, who had wisely decided to stay out of the war, recognised this as an opportunity. While the Greek states were quarrelling, he transformed Macedon into a state so strong that not only was it able to crush an alliance of Greek states, but was also soon confident enough to declare war on Persia. Philip was assassinated before seeing his plans fulfilled, but his son, Alexander, ensured that they came to pass, amassing the largest army ever to leave Greek soil.

Alexander the Great (356–323 BC)

Alexander III of Macedon, better known as Alexander the Great, united quarrelling Greek city states, conquered Egypt, defeated the Persians and united vast regions of Europe and Asia in the greatest empire the world had ever seen – all before the age of 33. By doing so he became one of the most admired leaders of antiquity. His armies were allegedly never once defeated, and Alexander was consequently recognised as a military genius.

To facilitate his desire to join the East and the West in one vast empire, Alexander adopted Persian dress, gave orders for Persians to be enlisted in his army, and encouraged his soldiers to marry Persian women. He also allowed conquered people to run their countries, provided they remained loyal to him. However, his continual warmongering eventually took its toll. When his army reached India in 326 BC, his troops, exhausted by years of battle, refused to go any further and Alexander was forced to head back home, only to die in Babylon three years later.

The Indian Mauryan Empire (321–185 BC)

When Alexander returned from India, he left a power vacuum into which stepped Chandragupta Maurya, the first emperor of the Indian Mauryan Empire. Chandragupta became the undisputed ruler of northern India and, for the first time in Indian history, gave the area a degree of political unity.

According to various sources, after ruling for some 25 years, Chandragupta became a monk and starved himself to death. His son Bindusara extended his empire, but it was Bindusara's son Ashoka who, after waging a brutal war of expansion against his enemies, gained remarkable fame in India through his conversion to Buddhism – a way of life that had gained many adherents since its introduction in the 6th century BC. Shocked by the aftermath of a major battle, Ashoka renounced all violence and then preached Buddhism and peace throughout his kingdom and abroad. Upon his death in 232 BC his family managed to hold on to power for another half century or so, until the last Mauryan emperor was murdered and India became divided once again. Periodically invaded, northern India would only become prosperous and stable again under the Gupta Empire in the 4th century AD.

Alexander's Successor Kingdoms

Alexander had not nominated an heir or successor, and although one person claimed the imperial legacy, it was rapidly sliced up by his key generals into numerous separate kingdoms that frequently waged wars upon each other. Of the two largest to remain, one was the Seleucid Kingdom – founded by Seleucus – which included most of Asia Minor, Mesopotamia and Persia.

The other was the Ptolemaic Kingdom of Egypt, founded by Ptolemy. With the exception of much of Persia, most of these lands and successor kingdoms were later swallowed by the Roman Republic.

Ptolemy established the last dynasty in Egypt, and would rule the country with the title of Pharaoh. For the following two and a half centuries the Greek Ptolemaic dynasty would successfully govern Egypt, mingling Greek traditions with the legacy of the Pharaohs. Ptolemy and his descendants adopted the trappings of Egyptian royalty and added Egypt's religion to their own, worshipping the gods and building temples in their honour, with some even going so far as to be mummified after death. Of all Alexander's successor kingdoms, the one in Egypt was to be the most long-lasting. It was only finally added to the Roman Empire in 30 BC, following the suicide of Cleopatra – the last Ptolemaic queen.

Buddhism

Buddhism is a philosophy[16] or way of life that originated in the 5th or 6th century BC (there is still disagreement about exactly when the Buddha lived). It is currently followed by over 300 million people.

Born into a royal family, Buddhism's founder, Siddhartha Gautama, realised that material wealth did not guarantee happiness, and left the comforts of his home at the age of 29 in order to understand the meaning of the suffering around him. After six years of study, meditation and self-denial, he is said to have awakened from the sleep of ignorance and become the Buddha, or 'the Enlightened One'.

For the following 45 years he taught the principles of Buddhism throughout northern India: if one lived a moral life, was mindful of one's actions, and developed wisdom, he taught, it was possible to dispel ignorance, rid oneself of desire and reach Nirvana – a state free of suffering.

His attempts at explaining injustice and inequality, and his teachings on how to avoid suffering, were met with a ready audience and spread rapidly around the world. Adopted by Ashoka in India in the 3rd century BC, Buddhism spread along the great trade routes from India into central and southeast Asia where it generally found favour, though it gradually became less popular in India itself.

---

[16] Buddhism is not centred around a god – hence the arguments about whether it is a religion or not – but rather around the importance of the teaching, or the Dharma. To its adherents, Buddhism goes beyond religion and is more of a philosophy or way of life.

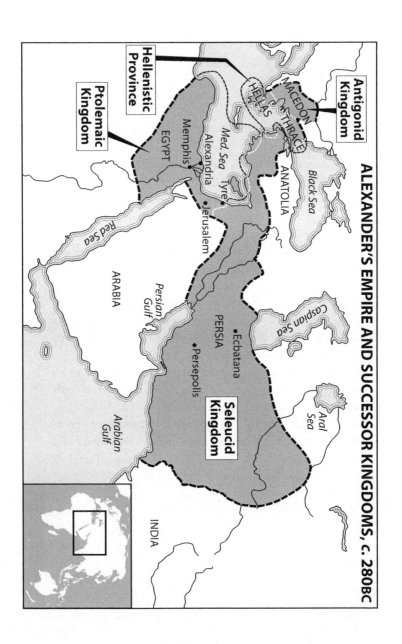

ALEXANDER'S EMPIRE AND SUCCESSOR KINGDOMS, c. 280BC

One of the many legacies of Alexander's reign was the city of Alexandria, which was founded on the northern coast of the country in the 4th century BC out of a desire to dominate Egypt. With Athens declining and Rome not yet ascendant, Alexandria occupied the key junction between the western and eastern worlds. It became one of the greatest cities in antiquity, the busiest port in the world and a cultural melting pot of Greek, Roman and Egyptian thought and trade. Around 200 BC, Eratosthenes, a Greek living in Alexandria, deduced that the world was a sphere, and even calculated its diameter with an accuracy that would not be surpassed for nearly 2,000 years. Another Greek, Aristarchus of Samos, claimed that the earth circled the sun, almost two millenia before Copernicus reached the same conclusion. Alexandria's importance within Egypt would not be eclipsed until Cairo was established in the 10th century.

The Unification of China (221 BC)

In the area now covered by present-day China, what had previously been a multitude of separate states were, by 400 BC, consolidated into a mere 13, and for the next 175 years they fell into a protracted struggle referred to as 'the Warring States Period'. The state that emerged as the strongest – whose iron weapons outmatched those of its bronze-dependent neighbours – was the western Chou state of Qin (pronounced Ch'in) from which, some have suggested, the name China is derived.

The leader who brought all these states together, and in effect became the first emperor of China in 221 BC, was named Shi Huang-Ti. He gained a terrible reputation for ruthlessly crushing any resistance to his rule. He also instigated the building of the Great Wall of China[17] – the largest man-made structure in the world at over 6,000 km long – in order to protect his empire from the Huns – the same people that would attack the West several hundred years later. Obsessed with immortality and fearing retribution by the spirits of all those he had killed, Shi Huang-Ti ensured that he was buried with over 6,000 terracotta warriors to protect him in the afterlife, making his burial site the largest on earth. The warriors were discovered only in 1974 by farmers digging a well.

As a result of his cruelty, the Qin Dynasty was rapidly overthrown after his death, and the Han Dynasty ruled China for the following 400 years.[18] This was a time of peace that witnessed the adoption of Confucianism – a way of life and a system of ethics expounded by Confucius and his followers since the 6th century BC – as the state philosophy. It was during the Han Dynasty that the great trade route of the Silk Road was established, allowing Asia to trade silk and other luxuries not only with Persia and India, but with a new empire that was gaining ground to the west. This empire would grow by conquest and assimilation to rule the western world: Rome.

The Roman Republic (509–27 BC)

Rome started as a small town on the banks of the river Tiber in the 8th century BC. Legend has it that the city was founded in 753 BC by the twins Romulus (hence Rome) and Remus, who were both saved from death by a she-wolf who suckled them. The area was ruled by Etruscan kings until 509 BC, when a more representative form of government was established

---

[17]   Other emperors would extend the wall.
[18]   The Han Dynasty fell in AD 220. China would be united again only in 581.

under the Republic of Rome. The Republic grew rapidly, wisely incorporating the peoples it conquered as 'citizens', as opposed to 'subjects' – a strategy which effectively reduced the likelihood of rebellion.

Rome was not without competition, however. The dominant power in the Mediterranean at the time was a Phoenician trading colony, founded in the 9th century BC on the north coast of Africa in modern-day Tunisia: Carthage. By the 3rd century BC, the Carthaginian Empire had grown to become the greatest naval power in the Mediterranean, stretching from northern Africa and Sicily to the southern Iberian Peninsula in present-day Spain.

Looking to expand its power base beyond the Italian mainland, Rome interfered in the Carthaginian sphere of influence. Over the course of 118 years, from 264 to 146 BC, the Roman and Carthaginian empires were engaged in a titanic struggle for control of the western Mediterranean both on land and at sea. The so-called Punic Wars – from *Peoni*, the Latin word for Phoenicians – drained both sides of money and manpower. While there were three major Punic Wars in total, the most famous of these was undoubtedly the second. This involved a full-scale invasion of Roman territory in which the Romans suffered a number of severe losses, and from which they only narrowly emerged victorious.

Hannibal and the Punic Wars (264–146 BC)

In 221 BC, the leadership of the Carthaginian forces in Iberia was passed from the mighty general Hamilcar Barca to his 25-year-old son, Hannibal. In the autumn of 218 BC he invaded Italy from the north, crossing the Alps in winter with a number of elephants and tens of thousands of men. Arriving in Italy, he smashed through each wave of Roman forces he

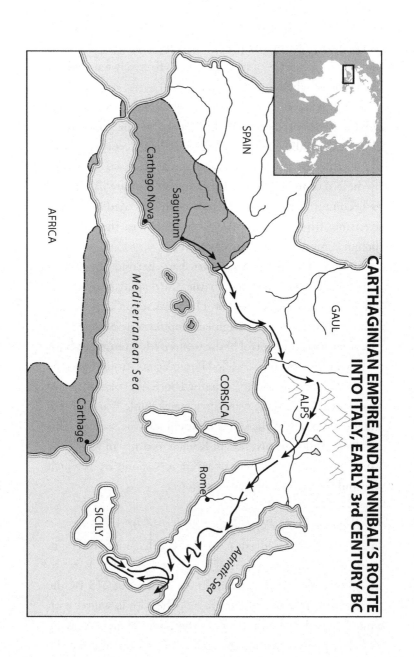

CARTHAGINIAN EMPIRE AND HANNIBAL'S ROUTE INTO ITALY, EARLY 3rd CENTURY BC

SPAIN

GAUL

AFRICA

Carthago Nova

Saguntum

Mediterranean Sea

Carthage

CORSICA

ALPS

Rome

SICILY

Adriatic Sea

encountered, conquering most of the north within two months, and causing several of the Republic's cities to rebel.

The Romans eventually retaliated by attacking Iberia, forcing much of the area to submit to their rule, before crossing into Africa and bringing the war to the gates of Carthage itself. The city sued for peace, and Hannibal was driven into exile, where he eventually killed himself. Carthage suffered the humiliation of becoming a dependent state, only to be razed to the ground by the Romans 50 years later following an attempt to reassert itself.

Rome now controlled the whole of the western Mediterranean, including northern Africa, and had grown from a minor regional power into an international empire. Its dominance was so unassailable that the Mediterranean became known to the Romans as *Mare Nostrum* or 'Our Sea'. Another victim of the Punic Wars was the kingdom of Macedon, whose king, Philip V, found his country under Roman occupation in 168 BC as punishment for supporting Carthage. Henceforth, the mighty Greeks of history became mere citizens of a Roman province.

Julius Caesar (100–44 BC)

A little under a century later, in 60 BC, we find Julius Caesar – already renowned for his exceptional oratory skills – taking the first steps along a path which would change Rome forever. Politically adept, Caesar formed an alliance known as 'the First Triumvirate', with Gnaeus Pompey – Rome's greatest general at the time – and Marcus Crassus, the city's richest man. With little opposition, they were able to split the empire into three separate power bases: Crassus would govern Syria, Pompey would govern Hispania (effectively the Iberian Peninsula), and Caesar himself took charge of northern Italy and south-east Europe, with southern Gaul later added.

Caesar's campaigns in Gaul (roughly modern-day France) between 58 and 50 BC only increased his fame; Caesar brought the local population under Roman control with a brutality that was notable even by Roman standards. The Gauls united under Vercingetorix – recognised today as the first national hero of France – with the aim of ejecting the Romans, but failed. By the time the war ended, according to the Greek historian Plutarch, up to a million Gauls lay dead and another million had been enslaved. Caesar also launched a minor invasion of the British Isles, but Britain would have to wait another hundred years before it felt the full force of Rome's might under Emperor Claudius (41-54).

Caesar's achievements upset the balance of power in Rome by threatening to eclipse those of Pompey. This instability increased when Crassus was killed – along with 30,000 of his men – when he attempted to invade neighbouring Parthia. The Parthians were a Persian tribe that had filled the power vacuum left by the weakening Seleucid Empire, and had subsequently become a major problem for the Romans.

Recognising Caesar as a potential threat, Pompey persuaded the Senate to order him back to Rome. Caesar did return, but not as a loyal soldier; instead he decided to wage war on an ungrateful republic. Caesar marched from Gaul to Italy with his legions, and crossed into Roman territory at the river Rubicon in northern Italy, which had served as the boundary between Rome and the provinces. If any general crossed it uninvited with an army, it was a sign that he entered Italy as an enemy. Since then, the phrase 'crossing the Rubicon' has survived to refer to any individual committing himself to a risky course of action.

Caesar's action sparked a civil war from which he emerged as the unrivalled leader of the Roman world. In response to Caesar's invasion, Pompey was appointed Commander-in-Chief of the Roman army with instructions to defeat his former ally, only to have his armies routed. With Caesar in hot pursuit, Pompey fled to Egypt and was assassinated on the orders of the pharaoh Ptolemy XIII, brother of Cleopatra. Before returning to Rome, Caesar was seduced by Cleopatra, who bore him a child, whom he named Caesarion. He also helped Cleopatra defeat her brother, with whom she had been forced into marriage and co-rulership, installing her as sole ruler.

Upon his return to Rome, Caesar's victories were celebrated. He was appointed dictator for ten years, and the Senate bestowed further honours on him, including a decree that the month of July be named after him[19] and that his image be stamped on coins – a traditional symbol of monarchy, and an action that did not go unnoticed among the notoriously anti-monarchical Romans.

Caesar was popular with the people as a reformer, but he was equally if not more unpopular with a number of senators who were keen to maintain the status quo and feared losing their wealth and power. It was these senators who conspired to murder Caesar under the pretext that they suspected him of trying to become king – reviving an institution that Rome had abolished in 509 BC. They succeeded in doing so on 15th March 44 BC, otherwise known as the Ides of March. The dagger thrust into Caesar's heart would equally wound the Roman Republic, plunging it into a succession of civil wars

---

[19] The month of August would be named after Emperor Augustus, who also declared himself a god.

that would end with its collapse and lead to the establishment of the Roman Empire.

Octavian, Mark Antony and Cleopatra

Before Caesar was murdered, he had appointed his grandnephew Gaius Octavius, known as Octavian, as heir to all he possessed, including his name. After much initial antagonism between Octavian and Mark Antony – Caesar's former right-hand man and an experienced soldier in his own right – the two joined forces to bring Caesar's murderers to justice.

However, the mutual distrust soon resurfaced between them. Antony's infatuation with the East and with Cleopatra, with whom he had three children, led to his final undoing and his vilification in Rome. Rumours circulated that he was celebrating victories in Alexandria as opposed to Rome; that he wanted to be buried there; and that he was bequeathing parts of the Roman Empire to Cleopatra and her children, including Caesarion – a bequest that effectively challenged Octavian's place as heir to Caesar.

Portraying Antony as an Egyptian pawn, Octavian declared war on Cleopatra and, by extension on Antony. The two forces met at Actium in north-west Greece in 31 BC, where Octavian won a decisive naval battle. The following year both Cleopatra – the last pharaoh of Egypt – and Antony took their own lives. Egypt, like Greece before it, became a Roman province.

The Roman Empire (27 BC – AD 476/1453)

The Roman Empire, as opposed to the Roman Republic, was founded in 27 BC when the Roman Senate bequeathed to Octavian the name Augustus, meaning the 'exalted' or 'holy one'. As a matter of course, Octavian also became *Princeps*

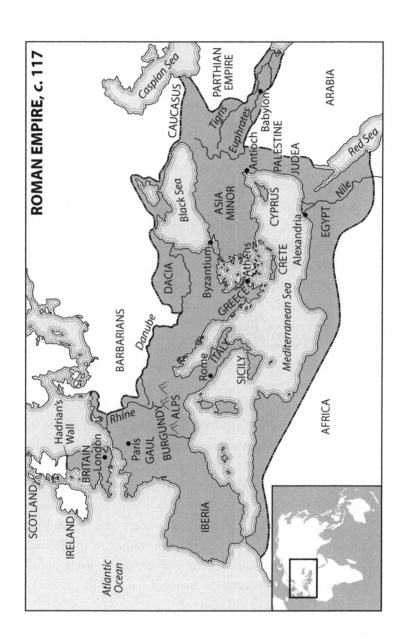

ROMAN EMPIRE, c. 117

Senatus, or leading man of the state. This later became the official title of the Roman emperors, and gave us the word 'prince'. One of his many titles, *Imperator* – initially awarded only to victorious generals – became particularly associated with the ruler, and was henceforth linked to leaders of empires (emperor, *empereur*, etc.).

Emperor Augustus Caesar ruled with absolute power. Any concerns diehard Republicans might have maintained about this were offset by the political and social stability that Augustus managed to introduce after decades of civil war. In fact, with the exception of a few minor interruptions and wars, and helped by the fact that Parthia – Rome's most significant potential enemy – was also beset by political turmoil, the Roman Empire was to know two centuries of relative peace, referred to as the *Pax Romana*. Trade was brisk. In addition to imports of wheat from Africa, wine from Gaul and oil from Iberia, spices and textiles were imported from Arabia, India and China by Asian caravans along the Silk Road.

A huge territory containing up to 50 million people, the empire was difficult to administer and expensive to maintain, requiring regular new sources of tax to fund its running costs. Augustus was fortunate that the state treasury received an influx of wealth and tax revenue from the newly occupied territory of Egypt, which became the breadbasket of the Roman Empire. A major economic revival – the result of prolonged peace and increased trade – also boosted tax revenues. In fact, there was enough money in the Roman coffers to allow Augustus to embark on a major public building programme and to boast: 'I found Rome a city of brick and left it a city of marble.'[20]

---

[20]   As quoted by the Roman historian, Suetonius.

The tax base may have increased, but it still needed to be collected. One of the ways of ensuring tax revenue was to perform a census that would confirm how many people lived in the empire and which of these could pay tax. According to the Christian New Testament, it was to register for such a census that Joseph and his wife Mary came to Bethlehem, a town in Judea in present-day Israel, where Mary gave birth to their son, Jesus.

Some Roman Emperors, Good and Bad...

The Roman Empire was run by a series of emperors, some better than others. Emperor Claudius launched a major invasion of England in AD 43 and managed to impose Roman rule in the south of the island that lasted some 350 years. Emperor Nero, on the other hand, had his mother and wife murdered; blamed the Great Fire of Rome in AD 64 on Christians, promptly throwing them to the lions, then eventually committing suicide.[21] Emperor Titus had to deal with both a terrible plague and with the eruption of Mount Vesuvius in AD 79, but nevertheless managed to open the Colosseum with 100 days of games.

After Titus' death in AD 81 until the end of the 2nd century AD, emperors adopted their successors as opposed to passing the crown down through family lines. This led to a succession of capable emperors, all of whom avoided civil war and contributed in some way to making Rome the dominant power in Europe. The appointment as emperor in AD 180 of Lucius Commodus, after the death of his father, Marcus Aurelius, was the first time a son had succeeded his father since

---

[21] It is believed that the apostles Peter and Paul were killed during this time.

AD 79. His reign was a disaster, and after his murder in AD 192, Rome faced a century of turmoil and anarchy.

Jesus: The Birth of Christianity

Jesus was born sometime between 6 BC and 4 BC. Very little is known about the man until he began his ministry at around the age of 30. At this time, Jesus began spreading a message of love and peace in a period when Judea was under the domination of an occupying Roman army. He challenged and angered the established Pharisee leaders, who successfully called for the Roman occupiers to crucify him for blasphemy. According to the Bible, he angered them specifically by his claims that he could forgive sins, which they believed only God could do.[22]

Jesus gained a group of Jewish followers, partly through his teachings, but also because many of them believed he was the Messiah – the great leader whose return was foretold in the Torah, and who would liberate his people and usher in a time of peace. His crucifixion in circa AD 28-29 was a catastrophe for his devotees. Shortly after his death, however, a large number of them claimed he had risen from the dead and had appeared to them. His resurrection became the basis of Christian belief from then on.

At the time of his crucifixion, Jesus' followers were nothing more than members of a small Jewish sect, occasionally persecuted by the Romans. In AD 380, however, with the Edict of Thessalonica, Christianity became the state religion of the Roman Empire. Today, Christianity is one of the major global religions, and has influenced legal and political systems around the world, as well as the western calendar, which is based around the birth of Christ.[23]

---

[22]   The Gospel of Luke 5:21: 'Who is this fellow who speaks blasphemy? Who can forgive sins but God alone?'

[23]   For many years, the numbering system of years was referred to as BC (Before Christ) and AD (Anno Domini), but many people now refer to the same period as BCE (Before the Common Era) and CE (the Common Era). They refer to the same dates.

The Decline of Rome

A single 50-year period in the middle of the 3rd century AD saw more than 20 emperors, with all but one either killed in battle or murdered by rival claimants to the throne. Torn apart by warring renegade armies and lacking strong leadership, Rome was brought to the point of collapse. When the empire stopped expanding, the flow of booty and slaves that had fuelled it for so long dried up, and the army – hitherto an enforcer of Roman might – became an expensive problem. Additionally, the civil war meant that many soldiers were moved from the frontiers in order to defend the empire against internal rebellion. This left the borders weakly defended, encouraging further attacks. Rome was also increasingly threatened by the rise of the Persian Sassanids, who sensed weakness in their neighbour.

Within the empire, commanders in the more remote provinces increasingly began to behave as independent rulers, paying scant attention to Rome. It was in response to such problems that the Emperor Valerian split the empire into two zones of responsibility, one in the east and one in the west. Yet in many ways this was too little too late. Thus, when Valerian marched eastwards in AD 260 to deal with the Sassanids, who had succeeded the Parthians, he was captured by their 'King of Kings', Shapur I, and died a prisoner, after allegedly suffering many indignities, such as being used by the Persian king as a mounting block before riding.

The combined cost of all the civil wars, conquests and subsequent troop relocation and garrisoning forced the emperors to look for new sources of income. They tried to levy further taxes on the lands they administered, but this only increased local resentment towards Roman occupation. That Rome was able to recover at all is attributed to the leadership of Emperor Diocletian who, after killing a rival claimant to the throne, was proclaimed emperor by his own troops in AD 284. Diocletian managed to institute reforms that brought an end to the terrible decades of war and civil unrest. Following the example of Valerian, he divided the empire geographically into East and West, which brought further stability. What Diocletian would probably not have anticipated was that the division of the empire along these lines would contribute to the eventual downfall of Rome.

Diocletian's plans for a smooth succession collapsed when the western emperor died, and his son, Constantine, claimed the throne for himself. In AD 312, Constantine invaded Italy to fight a rival claimant to the throne. After defeating his opponent at the battle of Milvian Bridge, Constantine professed to have seen a cross in the sky before the battle, accompanied by the words: 'In this sign you will conquer'. A year later, he signed the Edict of Milan – a proclamation of tolerance for all religions in the Roman Empire, including that of the Christian sect.

When yet more civil war erupted, in an attempt to maintain control, Constantine founded a new capital in the east on the site of the ancient Greek city of Byzantium, conveniently located between Europe and Asia, naming it after himself. Constantinople ruled the eastern half of the empire, and the city maintained its status as one of the greatest cities in the world for the next 1,000 years, while Rome languished and eventually collapsed.

Barbarians at the Gate

The main threat to the empire came not from the Persians, but from bordering barbarian tribes, such as the Goths, the Vandals and the Alans, which all began to encroach on Roman

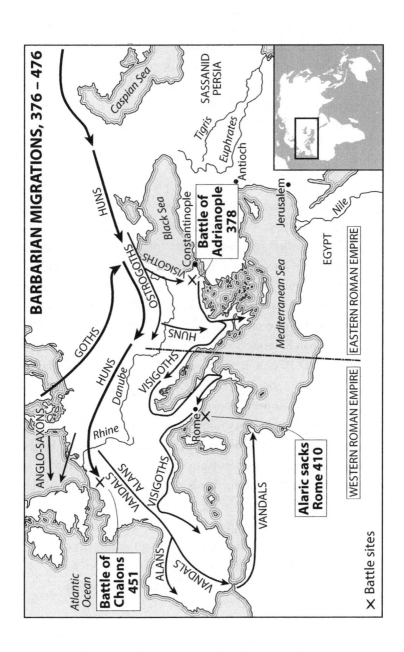

BARBARIAN MIGRATIONS, 376 – 476

territory. Traditionally, Rome had attempted to manage these tribes by paying off their leaders – especially during periods when they were concerned about internal threats – by trading with some, and by subjugating others. Barbarian warriors were often used as a source of manpower[24] to fight Rome's battles, both internal and external. Thus, it was a Vandal who had become a Roman general who sought to defend the Roman Empire against the invading Goths.

The situation became more pressing with the rise of the Huns. These nomadic livestock-herders from the great Eurasian Steppe – between the fringes of Europe and the western borders of China – were forced westward by three centuries of chaos in China, between roughly 300 and 600 AD, commonly referred to as the 'Age of Disunity'. Invading the lands of various Germanic tribes, the Huns conquered some and forced others to seek refuge within the confines of the Roman Empire.

In AD 376, a large group of Goths fleeing the Huns assembled at the river Danube, requesting permission from the Eastern Roman emperor, Valens, to move into Roman territory. Thinking they might serve both as a valuable supply of manpower in his war against the Persians and as a buffer against the new invaders from the east, Valens granted them permission to settle on lands near the Danube. However, the neighbouring Roman garrisons, unprepared for such a large number of immigrants, were not willing or able to share their precious food and supplies. Perhaps unsurprisingly, after two years this increasingly hungry and disaffected mass of barbarian troops eventually rebelled against their host.

---

[24]   After a defeat, it was customary for Rome's enemies to supply labour and food, and give a number of young men for service in the Roman army.

Accompanying his troops on the hundred-mile journey from Constantinople to Adrianople, Emperor Valens led his army into one of the greatest defeats ever suffered by the Roman Empire, and lost his life in the process. Such a crushing conquest by the Goths, and the death of the emperor at their hands, removed the Roman army's aura of invincibility, encouraging confidence in other less assertive Germanic barbarian tribes.

Emperor Theodosius – Valens' successor – attempted to pacify the Goths following the debacle of Adrianople by giving them lands in what is now Bulgaria. However, by using them as cannon fodder in his battles, he ultimately succeeded only in inflaming the situation. Under their leader, Alaric, the Goths rebelled in the early part of the 5th century, marching on Italy and sacking Rome – the heart of the western world – in AD 410.[25]

Likewise, encouraged by their new leader, Attila, the Huns continued their westward march, only retreating in AD 451 after being defeated deep in Gaul by a combined army of Romans and Goths. Attila died a few years later, and the subsequent struggle for succession destroyed the Hunnic Empire, which gradually dwindled into insignificance.

The End of the Roman Empire in the West (AD 476)

The Western Roman Empire managed to limp on until AD 476 when Germanic troops in Italy mutinied, electing as king a Gothic commander, Odoacer. He promptly deposed the emperor, Romulus Augustulus, and proclaimed himself king of Italy. And so, with more of a whimper than a bang, the

---

[25]   Alaric initially threatened to sack Rome in AD 408 and the city was saved only when it promised to pay 4,000 pounds of gold. When it refused to pay, the Goths made good on their threat.

Western Roman Empire came to an end. The Eastern Roman Empire – encompassing modern Greece, Turkey, northern Egypt and parts of the Middle East – lasted another thousand years, gradually being whittled away until Constantinople finally fell to invading Turks in AD 1453.

The Western Empire collapsed for several reasons. By overextending its geographic boundaries, it had insufficient troops to protect its lengthy borders. Moreover, communicating with such troops as there were – not to mention providing supplies and pay – proved difficult when horses were the fastest mode of transport at the time. The influx of barbarians from the east, and their corresponding land-grab, stripped the empire of the tax base that it had used to fund its armies. Quite apart from this, the administration of such a large politically and culturally diverse territory ultimately proved unsustainable. The lack of strong leadership – most notably in the 3rd century – only exacerbated these problems, leading to a series of civil wars, which undermined the empire and further weakened its borders.

The Eastern Empire by contrast, with its smaller defensible borders, larger population and greater wealth, proved much more manageable. Both its tax revenues and continued trade with the Orient enabled Constantinople to provide sufficient troops and civil servants for the defence and administration of its empire.

The Roman Empire at its height was the largest the world had ever seen. Romans were ruthless in their pursuit of victory, and captives were routinely slaughtered or trained as gladiators for the enjoyment of its citizens. Prisoners who did not die were enslaved, and slaves constituted a considerable portion of the population. But Rome also brought peace and order to a chaotic world. The Roman genius for engineering brought many benefits: roads to move troops, and aqueducts that provided populations with fresh water and public baths, to name but a few. Moreover, its legal and administrative traditions formed the basis for many Western governments that followed.

The Mayan Civilisation of Central America (AD 300–900)

As the Western Roman Empire was coming to an end, another great civilisation on the other side of the world, in Central America, was about to go through its golden age: that of the Mayans. The two empires never knew of each other.

Rising from the ashes of the collapsed Olmec civilisation, the Mayans were predominant in Central America for much of the first millennium. While never unified under one leader, they nevertheless constructed great stone buildings and pyramid-shaped temples. These formed the core of many city states, with populations ranging from several hundred to tens of thousands. Their largest city, Tikal, may even have had up to 100,000 inhabitants. They waged war on their neighbours, torturing and sacrificing prisoners of war in order to appease or nourish their gods – deities of the sun, the moon and the rain.

The Mayans developed several incredibly accurate calendars without the use of any scientific instruments. Obsessed with time-keeping, they were even able to predict solar eclipses. One of these calendars prophesied that doomsday – the end of the world – would occur on 21st December 2012. Happily, in this instance it was incorrect. However, an apocalypse of sorts did take place around 900 AD when, due to overpopulation, deforestation, drought or war, Mayan society went into rapid decline. Their cities were abandoned and eventually swallowed by the rainforest.

III

EARLY MIDDLE AGES

(AD 500 – 1000)

The Dark Ages (AD 500-800)
In Europe, the centuries that followed the fall of Rome were characterised by chaos, warfare, feuding, disease, illiteracy and superstition – not unlike what China had experienced at the end of the 3rd century. The loss of knowledge, the lack of written history and the general barbarity of this period in Europe has led to its most familiar designation: the Dark Ages. Historians, however, generally refer to it as the Early Middle Ages or Early Medieval period.

What little classical learning was retained owed its survival primarily to the Church, which was funded by contributions and land holdings. Not only had Christianity become the official state religion of Rome in AD 380, but many of the Germanic tribes had also become Christian, if only notionally, attracted by the religion's message of peace.

In the early 5th century, as Alaric was attacking Rome, British tribes had risen against their Roman occupiers, forcing them out of England after more than three centuries of foreign rule. Their freedom was short-lived, however: with the Romans gone, the island was overrun by Saxons, Angles, Jutes and other tribes from northern Germany and Denmark. These tribes replaced the indigenous population as the dominant social group and subsequently became known as the Anglo-

Saxons. Their various Germanic dialects merged to become Old English.

In mainland Europe, Germanic tribes, originally composed of small, scattered autonomous units, eventually became sufficiently organised to administer a larger area, and powerful enough to conquer their neighbours. By AD 500 a series of successor kingdoms stood in the place of the Western Roman Empire. The Vandals had built a kingdom in formerly Roman-occupied northern Africa; the Visigoths had taken over south-west Gaul and most of the Iberian Peninsula; the Burgundians had settled across south-east Gaul and the Franks in northern Gaul; the Anglo-Saxons had settled in Britain, the Alamanni in Eastern Europe, and the Ostrogoths in Italy.

It was the Franks, however, who developed the most prosperous successor kingdom in early medieval western Europe. They succeeded in uniting most of Gaul under their king, Clovis, after having overthrown the last Roman governor of Gaul. The Franks also drove the Visigoths south of the Pyrenees and started a new dynastic line – the Merovingians. By the time Clovis died in AD 511, the barbarian tribes in Gaul had merged into a Frankish superpower.

Byzantium: The Eastern Empire

With the demise of the Western Empire, Constantinople became the centre of the civilised world and, after centuries of leadership, Rome's power was essentially limited to part of the Italian Peninsula. The emperor in the East called himself the Roman Emperor (despite the fact that the main language at his court was Greek, not Latin) and the citizens of Constantinople still called themselves Romans. Yet the culture of the Eastern Empire was to become more and more dissimilar to that of Western Europe, blending Roman and Greek traditions with elements of Persian and Arabian culture. With time, its church refused to acknowledge the authority of Rome, recognising instead the Patriarchy of Constantinople, until it finally split from the Western Church completely, becoming the Greek Orthodox Church.

The Eastern or 'Byzantine' Empire – a term only coined by historians in the 16th and 17th centuries – controlled a significant area for the next several hundred years. While in the West the urban population declined, and the aqueducts and magnificent buildings built by the Romans became derelict and quarried for building material, the Empire in the East actually expanded.

In the 6th century, Emperor Justinian sought to revive the Roman Empire by invading Italy, the African coast and various parts of Spain, with no little success. By AD 542 the empire's extent was greater than it had been for more than two centuries. Justinian also introduced judicial reforms – including the complete revision of all Roman law – and building programmes which included the famous Hagia Sophia, the splendid basilica which would later become a mosque, and ultimately a museum in present-day Istanbul.

A devastating outbreak of bubonic plague in the early 540s marked the end of an age of splendour. The empire's population diminished substantially, with up to 50 percent of the population dying in a number of urban areas. Justinian himself is one of the lucky few who caught the plague but survived. Some historians believe that repeated instances of the plague over the following 200 years caused the death of up to 100 million people.

In addition to being weakened by plague, and having over-extended itself in the west, Byzantium was also constantly threatened in the east by Sassanid Persia – the only empire

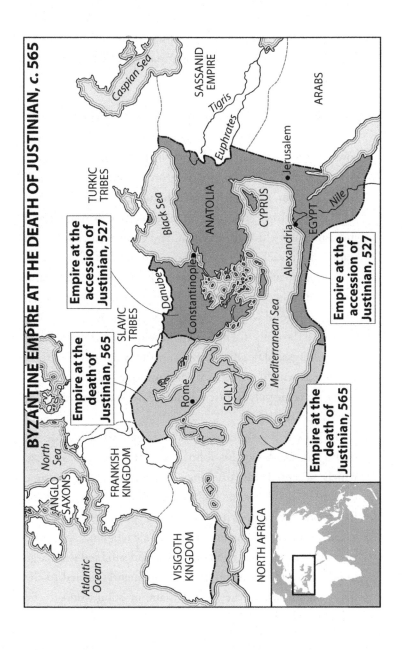

BYZANTINE EMPIRE AT THE DEATH OF JUSTINIAN, c. 565

Empire at the accession of Justinian, 527

Empire at the death of Justinian, 565

Caspian Sea

SASSANID EMPIRE

Tigris

Euphrates

ARABS

Jerusalem

TURKIC TRIBES

Black Sea

ANATOLIA

CYPRUS

Nile

Alexandria

EGYPT

Danube

Constantinople

Mediterranean Sea

SLAVIC TRIBES

Rome

SICILY

North Sea

ANGLO-SAXONS

FRANKISH KINGDOM

Atlantic Ocean

VISIGOTH KINGDOM

NORTH AFRICA

able to match its strength. A series of wars between the two empires in the early 7th century exhausted them both. Enfeebled and exposed, the two powers were no match for the encroaching Muslims.

Muhammad: The Last Prophet (AD 570–632)

In AD 610, at the age of 40, a trader-turned-prophet from the town of Mecca in Arabia, claimed he had seen visions of the Angel Gabriel while sleeping in a cave. Gabriel, he claimed, had told him to preach monotheism to the polytheistic Arab desert tribes. The existing religions of Christianity and Judaism, with which Muhammad had come into contact as a trader, also preached monotheism – the worship of one god.

Muhammad's simple message of the oneness of God, and the equality of all in His eyes – emphasising social justice, charity and good works – resonated with the poor. However, it angered the powerful merchant class in Mecca, who rejected his teachings and became actively hostile. Since much of their revenue depended on the city's pagan shrine – the Kaaba – an attack on their polytheistic religion represented an attack on Mecca's prosperity.

In AD 622, Muhammad was forced to leave Mecca, leading an exodus of his followers to the town of Medina, which accepted his teachings. Henceforth, this became known as the Hejira, or flight, and can be compared to the Exodus of the Hebrew tribes from Egypt under Moses as a turning point in the history of the Islamic religion. Eight years later, Muhammad marched on Mecca and subdued it. A large number of Arabian desert tribes subsequently turned to the new religion, which they called Islam, or 'submission to the will of God'.

When Muhammad died in AD 632, adherence to his fledgling religion was limited to these desert-dwelling tribes. Within a hundred years, however, Muslim armies controlled territory from Spain in the west and Africa in the south to Persia in the east, and had managed to subdue entire empires.

Common explanations for the success of the Muslim armies highlight the effects of plague and war. The pestilence that had ravaged both Sassanid Persia and Byzantium in the 6th century seems to have bypassed much of Arabia – its deserts may have acted as geographical barriers to the spread of disease, and its smaller population centres offered less scope for contagion. Hygienic reforms introduced by Muhammad also seem to have been highly effective. As for war, Persia and Byzantium had been so weakened by their incessant conflict that they were unable to withstand the might of conquering armies driven by religious zeal and attracted by the promise of a share in the spoils. In addition, communities weary of the oppression, corruption and burdensome taxes of the existing regimes welcomed the invaders.

However, the speed of the Islamic success masked underlying problems within the community. Most notably, Muhammad's failure to appoint a successor, or even establish a procedure by which a new leader might be chosen, resulted in differences of opinion as to who should succeed him. Muhammad's son-in-law, Ali – considered too young for the role – was passed over in favour of one of the Prophet's closest friends, Abu Bakr. This decision would later prove to be a major source of division across the Islamic community: one group became *Ahl Al-Sunna* – those who followed the Sunna, or way of the Prophet – while the followers of Ali launched *Shi'at'Ali* – the party of Ali – thereafter known as the Shiites.

Upon Muhammad's death Abu Bakr became caliph, or righteous heir, and was determined that all Arabs in the Arabian Peninsula should acknowledge the leadership of the Muslim community, even if this could only come about by force. He achieved his goal in a mere two years. Having brought the tribes together, he directed them against outside enemies. Thus began a bold series of campaigns, spreading out from *Dar al-Islam* – or the 'House of Islam' – into the lands beyond: *Dar al-Harb*, or the 'House of War'.

The Arab armies offered comparatively easy terms to those they defeated, especially to Jews and Christians, whom they termed 'people of the Book', and to whom they permitted freedom of worship. They also did not demand that conquered peoples convert to Islam: Muslims were not required to pay taxes, so more converts would have entailed smaller tax revenues. Essentially, as long as people accepted Arab sovereignty and paid taxes, they could continue to govern themselves.

When the third caliph, Uthman, was murdered 22 years after the death of Muhammad, the followers of Ali saw this as a chance to proclaim him as caliph. However, Ali was assassinated, and his son, Hasan renounced his claims to leadership – persuaded to do so by the existing Umayyad line – only to be later poisoned. When his brother, Husayn, subsequently sought power, he was murdered and his followers massacred, exacerbating the split between the Sunnis and the Shiites.

Over the next hundred or so years, Damascus, in present-day Syria, became the Islamic world's capital, presided over by the Umayyad clan, under whose leadership Muslims conquered vast tracts of land. To the east, Muslim armies successfully invaded Sassanid Persia and Central Asia, and gradually gained followers as far afield as India. To the west, in AD 711, a small army of northern African Berbers under Arab leadership – motivated by the promise of booty – invaded the Visigoth territory of Spain, conquering most of the Iberian Peninsula within a decade. From that point on, Spain became known as Al-Andalus – a peculiar hybrid of barbarian, Christian, Jewish and Islamic culture. The summit of the Rock of Gibraltar, known then by its Latin name, *Mons Calpe*, was renamed after the Moorish general, Tariq, as *Jabl Tariq* (the Hill of Tariq), from which the name Gibraltar is derived. Seven centuries would pass before the Muslims were driven from the peninsula entirely.

For many years the Islamic armies seemed unstoppable. A turning point in their expansion into north-west Europe came only in AD 732, when the king of the Franks, Charles Martel – otherwise known as 'Charles the Hammer' – and a coalition of troops under his leadership defeated an Umayyad army near Poitiers in France. While there is disagreement as to the size of this invading army, world history might have turned out very differently indeed had it not been defeated.

The Fall of the Umayyad Dynasty (AD 750)

Around that time, the Umayyads in Damascus were having to deal with difficulties of their own. The Umayyad Empire generated huge wealth for its rulers through trade and conquest, but decadent lifestyle of its rulers alienated the vast majority of their subjects. There was also increasingly vocal resentment that the booty of conquest was being held in Damascus and withheld from the men who carried out the actual fighting. Finally, the Arab-dominated Umayyad Dynasty found itself facing mounting demand for an Islamic rule where all Muslims would be equally represented.

This instability presented a perfect opportunity for the non-Arab Muslim and Shiite dissenters to encourage an uprising, and it was the Umayyads' efforts to quell it that led to their eventual downfall. Led by Abu l'Abbas al-Saffah – the great-great-grandson of the Prophet's uncle – the dissenters rebelled. They proclaimed Abu l'Abbas caliph and, in AD 750, having invited all the members of the Umayyad clan to a feast, slaughtered all but one of them. The sole survivor was Abd ar-Rahman, the grandson of a former caliph. He fled via Africa to Spain, where he defeated the governor of Al-Andalus, a supporter of l'Abbas, and established an independent emirate based in Cordoba.

Early African Empires

From the 7th century, the Muslims also explored much of Africa, many centuries before Europeans carved it up between themselves. Our knowledge of this continent's history is hampered by an absence of written records. The lack of a major transport infrastructure, such as that created by the Romans and the Chinese, makes its history very disparate. The fact that there is little archaeological evidence does not help things. We do know, however, that the growth of Carthage stimulated trade across the desert, and that this trade spread under the Romans, who named the continent after a tribe living near Carthage called the Afri.

It was Muslims who introduced the camel to the continent in significant numbers, further promoting trade and indirectly assisting the growth of regional powers such as the great West African empires of Ghana,[26] Mali and Songhai between the 7th and the 16th centuries.

---

[26]   Located in present-day Senegal and Mauritania, not in present-day Ghana, as the name might suggest.

Much of what we know about African states in the 14th century comes from the writing of Abu Abdalla Ibn Battuta. This famous 14th-century explorer spent almost 30 years travelling through the Islamic world, which then included northern Africa, India and Central Asia, China and the Middle East.

The Chinese Century (650 – 750)

While Europe was mired in darkness, China was very much at the forefront of global civilisation. After the collapse of the Han Dynasty in 220AD, it was not until 581 under the Sui Dynasty that much of China was once again united. While this dynasty was short-lived, it laid the foundations for one of the longest-enduring empires in Chinese history and possibly the greatest of the medieval world: the Tang Dynasty (618-907).

With enlightened leadership, and powerful, efficiently run armies that subdued its neighbours in the north and northwest, China thrived. The cultures and religions of Central Asia, the Middle East and Persia were absorbed by the court, with tourists and commerce flooding into the capital, Chang'an (modern day Xi'an), which rapidly became the largest city in the world. Such were the advancements in art, literature and poetry that the early 8th century is commonly regarded as the Golden Age of Chinese history. It was also during this time that tea became established as the national drink of China.

The Tang Dynasty suffered numerous natural disasters and, like the Sui dynasty that preceded it, became less tolerant and more divided, eventually subsiding into anarchy and collapsing completely.

The Islamic Golden Age (8th–11th Centuries)

In the Middle East, the new Islamic dynasty came to be known as the Abbasid Caliphate and is synonymous with the golden age of Islam. The Abbasids moved their capital from Damascus to Baghdad, and through trade with the East and its considerable agricultural wealth, this city soon became one of the richest in the world. It remained the political and cultural capital of the Islamic world from that time until the Mongol invasion in 1258.

Great wealth encouraged the Abbasids to support learning and the arts: under a succession of caliphs in the 8th and 9th centuries – the most significant being al-Mansur, al-Rashid and al-Mamoun – considerable efforts were directed towards gathering knowledge from around the world. As a consequence, the caliphate enjoyed a spectacular flowering of Muslim culture and intellectual achievement between the 9th and 11th centuries.

During this period, Islamic lands were richer and more open, cultured and sophisticated than any kingdom in the West, where non-religious learning was still considered suspect. As William Bernstein describes in *A Splendid Exchange*: 'The Arabs, invigorated by their conquests, experienced a cultural renaissance that extended to many fields; the era's greatest literature, art, mathematics, and astronomy was not found in Rome, Constantinople, or Paris, but in Damascus, Baghdad and Cordova.'[27]

The Abbasids encouraged study of the writings of the ancient Greek world. Caliph al-Mamoun opened the *Bayt al-Hikmah*, or 'House of Wisdom', where scholars from different lands gathered and studied. Books on mathematics,

---

[27] *A Splendid Exchange* by William Bernstein, Atlantic Books Ltd, 2008.

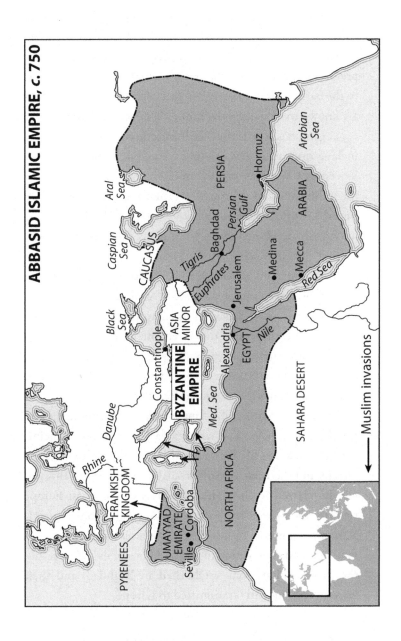

ABBASID ISLAMIC EMPIRE, c. 750

meteorology, mechanics, astronomy, philosophy, medicine and many other subjects were translated into Arabic from languages including Hebrew, Greek and Persian, thereby preserving ancient texts that were then of little or no interest to the barbarians in the West. In fact, a number of these works are known to us today only through Arabic translations.

Legend has it that the Muslims acquired the art of paper making from a Chinese artisan captured in battle in the mid-8th century. Whether or not this is true, paper was clearly in use in Muslim lands by the 8th century, and this further aided the rapid spread of ideas and knowledge. Indeed, a thriving book trade developed there, while many Europeans were still writing on animal skins or even bark.

The commands of the Qur'an fuelled the need for many inventions. For example, Muslims were required to pray to Mecca five times a day. In order to do this, they needed to know the time, and the direction in which to pray – information that could only be gained through scientific enquiry. Improvements in map-making and navigation were just two of the many consequences of this.

In the 11h century, Ibn Sina – a Persian writer known in the West as 'Avicenna' – wrote a vast treatise on medicine, bringing together all the medical knowledge of the ancient Greeks and the Islamic world available at that time. This was widely referred to in medical facilities of Christian Europe right up until the 17th century. As Jonathan Lyons explains: 'Koranic injunction to heal the sick spurred developments in medicine and the creation of advanced hospitals.'[28] As a result, the first hospitals were established in Baghdad, and their learning subsequently transmitted to Europe.

---

[28] *The House of Wisdom* by Jonathan Lyons, Bloomsbury edition.

The Islamic culture that developed on the Iberian Peninsula also attracted scholars from the East and 'the Muslim Emirate of Al Andalus, with its capital at Cordoba, became the most prosperous, stable, wealthiest and most cultured state in Europe.'[29] Indeed, much of the ancient wisdom of the Muslim world passed to the rest of Europe through what is now Spain.

Charlemagne (AD 742–814)

Meanwhile, in western Europe, the Frankish kingdom reached its apogee under the grandson of Charles Martel, Carolus Magnus, better known by his Gallic name, Charlemagne. Crowned sole king of the Franks in AD 771 at the age of 29, he is often recognised as the greatest king of the European Early Middle Ages, uniting the Frankish tribes and kingdoms in the West into the largest European empire since Rome. This empire included much of present-day France, Germany, the Netherlands, Belgium, Switzerland, Austria, Poland and Italy.

Charlemagne was rewarded for providing assistance to the pope on more than one occasion by being crowned Roman emperor in Saint Peter's Basilica in Rome on Christmas Day in AD 800. Although Charlemagne reigned for 46 years, his empire was short-lived: his son split it into three parts – one for each of his own sons. This resulted in an empire divided into numerous feudal states, threatened by enemies on its frontiers – Muslims to the south, Slavs to the east and Vikings to the north. One of Charlemagne's accomplishments, however, was to plant the seed of the idea of a renascent Roman Empire.

While his immediate successors failed to do justice to the title, the coronation of the German king, Otto I,

---

[29]   *Worlds at War* by Anthony Pagden, Oxford Press.

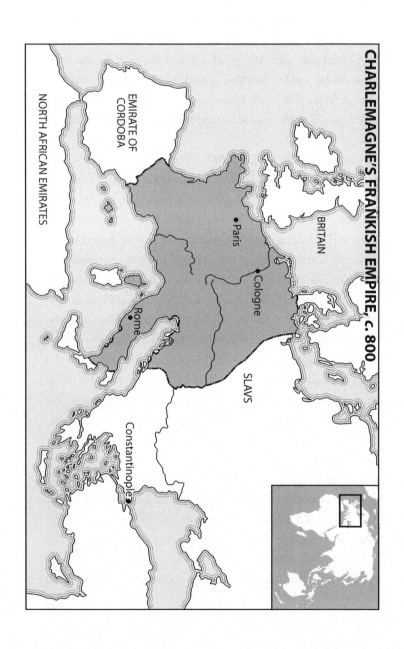

CHARLEMAGNE'S FRANKISH EMPIRE, c. 800

NORTH AFRICAN EMIRATES

EMIRATE OF CORDOBA

BRITAIN

Paris

Cologne

Rome

SLAVS

Constantinople

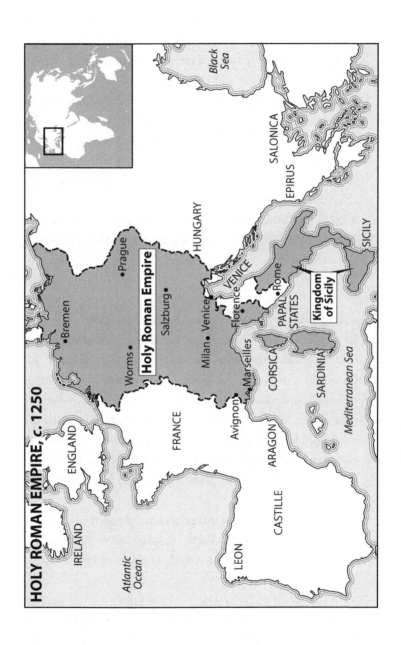

HOLY ROMAN EMPIRE, c. 1250

Black Sea

SALONICA

EPIRUS

HUNGARY

Prague

Bremen

Holy Roman Empire

Worms

Salzburg

VENICE

Milan Venice

Rome

Florence

PAPAL
STATES

SICILY

Kingdom
of Sicily

CORSICA

SARDINIA

Marseilles

Avignon

ARAGON

Mediterranean Sea

FRANCE

ENGLAND

IRELAND

Atlantic
Ocean

CASTILLE

LEON

by Pope John XII[30] in AD 962 marks the beginning of an unbroken line of emperors that lasted for the next eight centuries, nominally ruling a territory encompassing most of present-day Germany and parts of Italy. In 1157, Frederick I added the word 'Holy' to 'Roman Empire', in recognition of his role as defender of the faith.

All subsequent German sovereigns, ruling over a confederation of hundreds of independent entities, large and small, held this rank. The largest of these ruling families was the Austrian House of Habsburg, who possessed the title from 1452 until 1806. Looking back on the Empire, however, the 18th-century Enlightenment philosopher Voltaire rightly commented that it was 'neither Holy, nor Roman nor an Empire'.

Viking and Norman Invasions (AD 793–1066)

In AD 793, while Charlemagne was doing his best to rule his vast European kingdom, and while the Abbasid Caliphate was blossoming in the East, a group of sea warriors – or Vikings – from Scandinavia landed on the small island of Lindisfarne off the east coast of England. After mercilessly butchering the local population and robbing the monastery of its treasures, they departed. This marked the beginning of numerous raids throughout Europe that gradually grew in both magnitude and frequency.

The Vikings' key advantage was the element of surprise: their boats had shallow keels, allowing them to penetrate farther up rivers than other vessels of the time. Yet not only

---

[30] Pope John XII was one of the biggest scoundrels in history. In 963 Otto called a Church synod which found John XII guilty of murder, adultery, incest and perjury amongst other crimes. You can read more in my papal history: Pontifex Maximus.

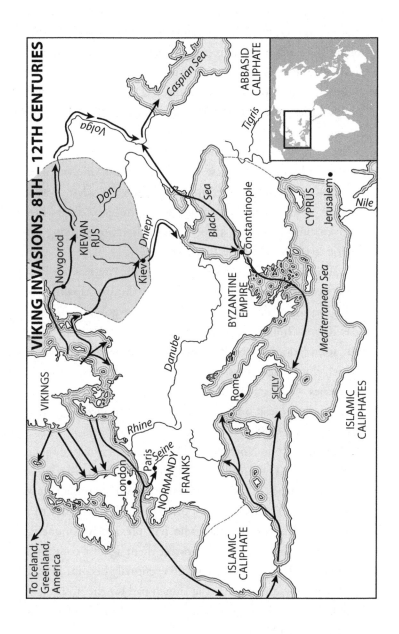

VIKING INVASIONS, 8TH – 12TH CENTURIES

were they skilled fighters and sailors, but also explorers, traders and settlers. In their wanderlust, they travelled farther afield than any other Europeans, discovering Greenland and Iceland, and even establishing a short-lived settlement on the northeast coast of America around AD 1000. Thus, it was the Vikings, not Columbus, who were the first Europeans to land in America. In general, those travelling west – from what is now Denmark and Norway – were driven by the desire for loot and conquest. By contrast, those who ventured south – predominantly from what is now Sweden – were mostly seeking trade, venturing down the great rivers that conveniently flowed in a north-south direction, linking the Baltic to the Caspian and Black Seas.

Those travelling south were known to the Arabs as the 'Rus', and were instrumental in establishing the principalities of Kiev in present-day Ukraine and Great Novgorod in present-day Russia. The development of trade around these cities laid the foundations of the Russian nation. In particular, Kiev – which dominated the state of Kievan Rus for the next two centuries – had trade links with Constantinople that played a significant role in bringing the Eastern Orthodox religion to the area in AD 988.

Vikings from Norway established a Norse kingdom in Ireland, and a few decades later Danish conquerors settled in eastern England. In the face of persistent Viking onslaught in AD 911, the Franks offered a bribe of further territory to a Viking leader named Rollo, who had previously conquered parts of northern France, to protect them against continued incursions. This gift of land would eventually become known as Normandy, and serve as the launch pad for the invasion of England by Rollo's great-great-great grandson, William the Conqueror, in 1066.

King Alfred[31] of England defended his island nation valiantly in the 9th century, but the Anglo-Saxons were ultimately so weak that the Danish king, Canute, was eventually able to combine the crowns of Denmark, Norway and England, creating a large northern empire during the early part of the 11th century.

However, as with most over-extended empires, that of Canute became too large for his successors to manage. Thus, when a Viking invasion force tried to invade northern England after the death of King Edward in 1066, it was defeated at the Battle of Stamford Bridge and expelled. Unfortunately for the English, this battle in the north took place in the same month as the attack on the south of England by the Normans. Having defeated the Danes at Stamford Bridge, Edward's successor, King Harold, had to rush 200 miles south to Hastings in order to defend the island against William, the Duke of Normandy, who came to claim the English throne. Had the two invasions not occurred within one month of each other, a stronger, less exhausted English army might have succeeded in repelling the Normans. But they didn't. Harold was allegedly struck in the eye by an arrow, the English were defeated, and a battle involving only a few thousand men changed the course of English history. Duke William has been known as 'William the Conqueror' ever since.

England was henceforth ruled by the Normans, who built a network of castles across the country to consolidate their power. They were not popular: they spoke French, followed Frankish and Viking customs, and set aside huge tracts of useful agricultural land for hunting. On mainland Europe, however, their renowned fighting skills endeared them to any

---

[31] King Alfred was the only English king to earn the epithet 'the Great'.

ruler willing to pay for armed assistance. In one instance, they were engaged by the pope to free Sicily and Southern Italy from Islamic domination, thereby gaining Sicily as a Norman kingdom for several generations.

IV

LATE MIDDLE AGES

(AD 1000 – 1500)

Challenges to the Caliphate
The golden age of the Abbasid Caliphate did not last long. The extravagance of its court caused many rifts, as did the embracing of Sunni Islam – the Abbasids had, after all, come to power with the support of Shiite Muslims. This alienated the loyalty of many, and led to the emergence of several regional centres of Islamic power which would ultimately challenge the central authority of the Caliphate.

The Umayyad prince who had fled to Spain after the massacre of his family represented only one disenchanted party. Many Shiites, believing the Abbasids to be usurpers, left for northern Africa. Here they established rival kingdoms, the most renowned of which was that of the Fatimids, who claimed descent from Muhammad's daughter, Fatima. Proclaiming a rival caliphate in AD 910, they conquered Egypt in AD 969, founding the city of Cairo as their capital, from which they ruled most of northern Africa.

By the 11th century, the Fatimids were already more powerful than the Abbasids in Baghdad. However, their gradual encroachment on Palestine and Syria brought them into direct conflict with both the Seljuk Turks and the invading European crusaders, which ultimately led to their downfall.

The Seljuk Turks had migrated to Persia from the Central Asian Steppe in the 11th century, settling in Abbasid lands and converting to Sunni Islam. Exploiting the weakness of the Abbasids, they gained control of Baghdad in 1055 and within 20 years had captured most of Asia Minor from the Byzantines, naming it the Independent Sultanate of Rum[32] after the Arabic word for Rome. This became the first permanent settlement of Turks in Asia Minor, and is generally understood to be the beginning of Islam in Turkey – the land of the Turks.[33]

Europe's Religious Schism (AD 1054)

While the Seljuks were conquering Asia Minor, Europe was suffering from its own religious fracture. For much of the Early Middle Ages there had been dwindling contact between the papacy in Rome and the patriarchy in Constantinople, both of which were administered separately. Numerous minor sources of discord had arisen over the years, such as the seemingly trivial matter of whether priests should have beards. These had caused a degree of alienation, but two issues drove a more formidable wedge between the churches. One was the claim to supremacy of the pope in Rome over all other bishops of the Catholic Church. This was robustly challenged by the Orthodox Church in the East. The other related to the significance and role of the Holy Spirit within the Christian Trinity – that is, the union between God, Jesus and the Holy Spirit.

Cultural and linguistic differences only intensified mis-understandings and increased alienation between the two groups, but the rupture became complete in 1054, when the

---

[32]   The Seljuk leader was awarded the title of Sultan from the Abbasid Caliph, becoming the first Muslim ruler to use the title.

[33]   The Seljuks also conquered Syria and Palestine from the Shiite Fatimids.

pope in Rome and the patriarch in Constantinople ex-com-municated each other. Ever since then, the Roman Catholic Church in the west and the Orthodox Church in the east have remained divided, not recognising the validity of the other's sacraments. Although attempts at reconciliation were made at various times – specifically during the advances of the Turks in the 14th and 15th centuries – they were unsuccessful. Very recently, however, there have been renewed hopes of a rap-prochement.

In the West, the Church had its own problems. In a superstitious world, the Church's power rivalled that of temporal rulers. With this power came wealth, and it soon became apparent that the new kings of Europe coveted both. When the emperors of the newly founded, and predominantly German, Roman Empire started making senior ecclesiastical appointments, the Church's response was to insist that bishops and abbots could only be appointed by the office of the pope.

To press the point home, and as punishment for daring to challenge him, the pope then excommunicated the German emperor, Henry IV. A bizarre sequence of events ensued: Henry elected another pope and Henry's enemies elected another emperor; Henry IV stormed Rome, prompting the pope to request help from the Normans, who proceeded to sack Rome themselves! The emperor and the pope were not reconciled until 1122, when it was finally agreed that while the emperor could not appoint bishops, he could nevertheless retain the right to grant them land. The whole episode became known as the 'Investiture Controversy'.[34]

---

[34] Should you be interested in this conflict and the history of the popes generally, please see *Pontifex Maximus*, my short history of the popes.

The Crusades (AD 1096–1291)

The encroachment of the Seljuk Turks from the east threatened not only pilgrim access to the Holy places but also Christendom itself, provoking increasing alarm in Europe in the mid-11th century. Indeed, the emperors in Constantinople had implored the pope on numerous occasions to assist them in repelling the heathens from the east. The Church in Rome now saw an opportunity not only to reaffirm its power, which had been increasingly challenged, but also to heal the rift between Roman and Orthodox Christianity.

And so, in 1095, Pope Urban II called for a 'crusade' to liberate Jerusalem from the infidels, even promising the forgiveness of sins as a reward for participation. Tens of thousands of people – the rich and poor of Europe, seeking adventure, wealth and land, or simply the guarantee of salvation – took up arms and headed east.

A large army of peasants was the first to set off, plundering central Europe and shamefully butchering thousands of Jews on the way. Few made it as far as Nicaea, only to be slaughtered by the Turks. During the same year, however, better-organised groups led by prominent nobles and professional soldiers arrived at Constantinople, sacking the Seljuk cities of Nicaea and Antioch on their way to Jerusalem.

When the Fatimids of Egypt heard of the fall of Antioch, they invaded Palestine and captured Bethlehem. Fortunately for the crusaders, the Seljuks and the Fatimids were sworn enemies, and consequently spent more time fighting each other than preparing for the defence of Jerusalem. Hence, in 1099, not long after the crusaders had entered Bethlehem, this invading army of French and Norman knights also took Jerusalem. Most of its population, regardless of religion, was butchered without mercy.

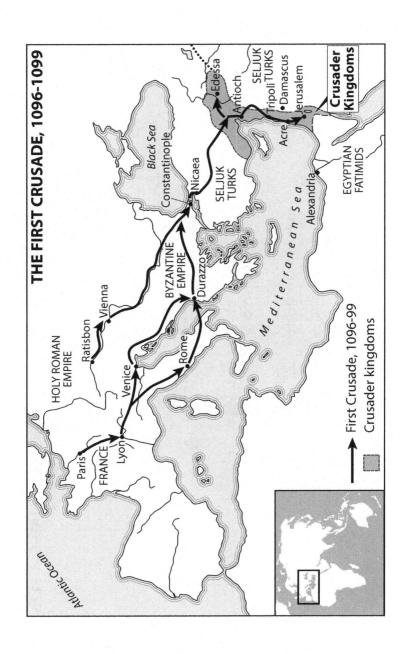

THE FIRST CRUSADE, 1096-1099

Atlantic Ocean

Paris
FRANCE
Lyon
Venice
Rome
HOLY ROMAN EMPIRE
Ratisbon
Vienna

Black Sea
Constantinople
Nicaea
BYZANTINE EMPIRE
Durazzo

SELJUK TURKS

Mediterranean Sea

Alexandria
EGYPTIAN FATIMIDS

Edessa
Antioch
SELJUK TURKS
Tripoli
Damascus
Jerusalem
Acre

Crusader Kingdoms

First Crusade, 1096-99
Crusader kingdoms

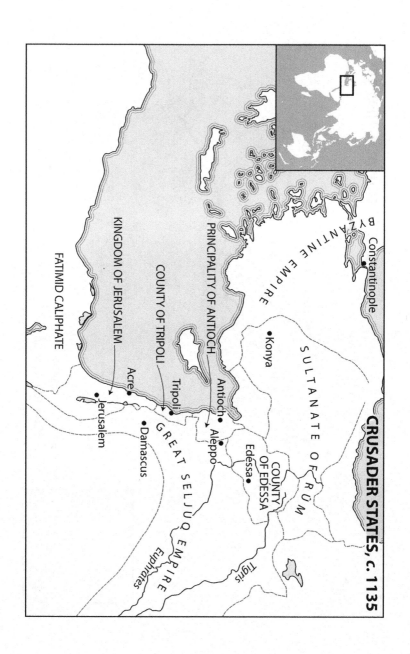

CRUSADER STATES, c. 1135

BYZANTINE EMPIRE

Constantinople

SULTANATE OF RÛM

Konya

FATIMID CALIPHATE

KINGDOM OF JERUSALEM

COUNTY OF TRIPOLI

PRINCIPALITY OF ANTIOCH

Acre

Jerusalem

Tripoli

Antioch

Aleppo

Damascus

Edessa

COUNTY OF EDESSA

GREAT SELJUQ EMPIRE

Euphrates

Tigris

Over the following years, four crusader kingdoms were founded in the heart of *Dar al-Islam*. Several huge forts were built to protect the crusaders, some of which still stand today. These kingdoms became known collectively as *Outremer*, from the French word for 'overseas', as most of the knights who had taken part in the first crusade were French or Norman. Many crusaders returned home after having fulfilled their vows, leaving the new kingdoms relatively undefended. This was partially solved by the foundation of the Knights Templar. This military order was established to protect both the crusader kingdoms and any pilgrims wishing to visit the newly liberated Jerusalem. Despite their best efforts, however, they were unable to protect one of the kingdoms (Edessa), which was taken by the Turks in 1144. A new crusade was launched to take it back, this time led by King Louis VII of France and King Conrad III of Germany, but it ended in disaster

Things took a further turn for the worse for the crusaders towards the end of the 12th century when the Muslim world of Egypt, Syria and much of northern Africa became united under the leadership of one man. This Sunni Muslim, Yusuf ibn Ayyub, would become known as Salah al-Din (Saladin), or 'Rectifier of the Faith'. Saladin founded his own dynasty: the Ayyubids.[35] Setting his sights on freeing the Holy Land from crusader rule, Saladin and his armies swept through the crusader kingdoms, taking city after city until Jerusalem itself finally fell back into Muslim hands in 1187 after a fortnight's siege. Saladin gained fame for sparing the inhabitants of the newly fallen city, in sharp contrast to the way the Christians had treated its occupants during the First Crusade.

---

[35]   The Fatimid Dynasty came to an end under Saladin.

With Europe in shock, Pope Gregory VIII quickly called for a third crusade – a call that was greeted with enthusiasm by Emperor Frederick Barbarossa of Germany, King Richard I of England[36] and King Philip II of France. This crusade was dogged by discord and bad luck: Frederick Barbarossa drowned in a river and most of his army returned home after his death; Philip II abandoned the crusade after a disagreement, taking his troops with him. Only Richard I reached the walls of Jerusalem, where he was advised by the Knights Templar that even if he succeeded in capturing the city, he would not have the manpower to hold it.

Frustrated by this turn of events, Richard resolved to return to England, where his brother, John – in whose hands he had left the throne while on crusade – was undermining his rule.[37] But before Richard left the Holy Land, he signed a peace treaty with Saladin which permitted the crusader kingdoms to retain much of their land. Christian pilgrims would also be granted access to Jerusalem, whilst the city itself would remain under Muslim control.

In 1203-4 yet another crusading army brought shame upon itself. The son of the deposed Byzantine emperor bribed them to help him retake his throne in Constantinople, but when he reneged on the deal, the furious crusaders rampaged through Constantinople, ransacking the city and butchering its population. Laden with treasure, instead of going on to liberate Jerusalem, the crusading army retuned home. This

---

[36] Richard's bravery on the Third Crusade earned him the epithet of 'Lionheart'.

[37] John's unpopular rule after Richard's death in 1199 eventually forced upon him the signing of the Magna Carta in 1215. The Magna Carta was a document, signed by the king, agreeing that his will was not arbitrary. It became the basis for citizens' rights.

single act dashed any hope of reconciliation between the Roman and Orthodox Churches.

Further crusades were launched over the next hundred years, one of which resulted in a 15-year occupation of Jerusalem. But patience with the crusader armies was eventually exhausted, and in 1261 the Byzantine Emperor drove them from Constantinople. By this time, however, the Byzantine Empire was just a fraction of its original size, occupying only parts of Greece and the north-west area of present-day Turkey. So, the remaining crusaders lingered on in Syria and Palestine in their protective forts, with their last fortress eventually falling to an invading Mamluk army in 1291.

The Mamluks: Kingdom of Slaves (AD 1250–1517)

Mamluks – from the Arabic *Mamluk* meaning 'enslaved' – first appeared under the Abbasid Caliphate. With their power already in decline, mistrustful of those surrounding them, and fearful of the bordering Byzantine Empire, in the 9th century the Abbasids had created an army loyal only to themselves. They achieved this by taking the sons of enslaved non-Muslim families, bringing them up as Sunni warriors and giving them positions of responsibility in the service of the caliphate. These slaves grew so powerful that they would eventually play a major role in the medieval Islamic world, overthrowing the remains of Saladin's Ayubbid dynasty in 1250[38] and quickly extending their authority over Palestine and Syria.[39]

---

[38] Ironically, it was the Ayyubids who had brought many of the Mamluks to Egypt in the first place.

[39] Ultimately, they fell before the onslaught of another Turkish force, the Ottomans, in 1517.

Although the crusaders were ultimately ejected from the Holy Land, the West had nevertheless reaped certain benefits: 'Although they would ultimately end in failure, the Crusades nonetheless paid significant dividends by bringing the Latin world face to face with the scientific and technological prowess of the Arab East.'[40] One of the skills the crusaders brought home with them was that of stone carving, which would greatly enhance the magnificent churches built throughout Europe in the 12th and 13th centuries. Another major effect of the Crusades was economic: the old Middle East and Asia were opened to the West, stimulating demand for Asian luxuries and turning Venice and Genoa into important trade centres. This in turn laid the foundations for the economic prosperity that would help drive the Renaissance in Europe.

While the Holy Land was in turmoil, Europe had enjoyed a period of peace. Agricultural advances had improved productivity, so that fewer farmers were needed to feed populations. More people moved to towns, and trade grew significantly as a result. However, this was all to be interrupted in the 13th century when Europe and the Middle East were invaded by new hordes of bloodthirsty warriors from the east: the Mongols.

The Mongols and Genghis Khan (13th – 15th Centuries)

An obscure pastoral and tribal people who lived in what is now Outer Mongolia, the Mongols had gradually unified towards the end of the 12th century. One of their leaders, Timuchin, so impressed them with his military abilities that in 1206, at the age of 42, he was named 'Universal Ruler' or Genghis Khan.

---

40   *The House of Wisdom* by Jonathan Lyons, Bloomsbury edition.

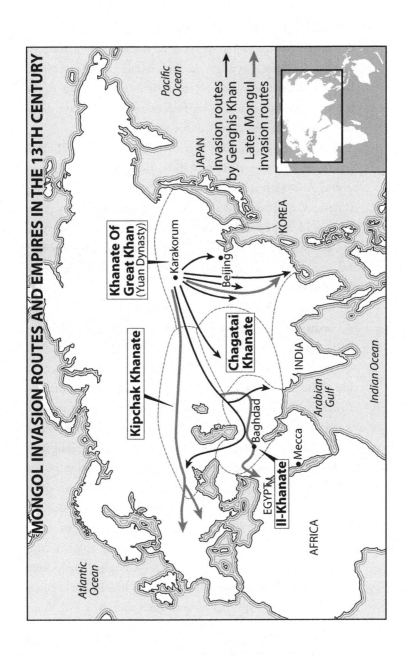

MONGOL INVASION ROUTES AND EMPIRES IN THE 13TH CENTURY

Pacific Ocean

JAPAN

Invasion routes by Genghis Khan

Later Mongul invasion routes

Khanate Of Great Khan (Yuan Dynasty)

Karakorum

Beijing

KOREA

Kipchak Khanate

Chagatai Khanate

INDIA

Baghdad

Arabian Gulf

Indian Ocean

EGYPT

Mecca

Il-Khanate

AFRICA

Atlantic Ocean

Under his leadership, the Mongols exploded out of the Steppe to terrorise much of Asia. Reasons for their westerly march are unclear: changes in the climate may have forced them to seek out new pastures for their animals, or new-found freedom from internecine warfare might simply have given them more time and energy to focus on adventuring.

Their success is perhaps slightly easier to explain. Ranged against them was a divided China, the disparate armies of central Asia with no single leader to rally them, a declining Abbasid Caliphate, and the series of fragmented city-states that would only become Russia in the 16th century. The world was, essentially, open for the taking. Their lightning mobility and spectacular horsemanship, alongside the discipline of their military machine, made the Mongols hugely successful. By the time of Kublai Khan, half a century or so later, they had managed to bring almost the entire Asian landmass under their control.

Genghis Khan died in 1227, aged around 65. Under the rule of his descendants, the Mongols occupied all northern China and overran much of Kievan Rus, destroying most of its major cities in the process. They then defeated the Seljuk Turks[41] before heading westwards into Poland and Hungary.

Then, while in the process of crossing the Danube and approaching Vienna, in December 1241, the Mongols quite mysteriously retreated. This may have seemed miraculous to the Europeans, but the Mongol withdrawal did not come about through divine intervention. Rather, their retreat was prompted by the death of Ogedei, Genghis Khan's son: Mongol nobles were required to return home in the event of their ruler's death in order to confirm a successor. Following

---

[41] The Seljuk Turks became vassals of the Mongols and, by the 14th century, their power was extinguished.

a short reign by one of Ogedei's sons in 1251, the position of Great Khan passed to Mongke, another of Genghis Khan's grandsons. Mongke continued the invasion of China, whilst sending his brother, Hulegu, westwards to bring the Abbasid Caliphate into submission.

In 1258, Hulegu rode into Baghdad, which until then was dominated by the Seljuk Turks, and unleashed his hordes upon the city. According to some estimates, up to 800,000 Muslims were massacred, including the last reigning Abbasid caliph – albeit one of vastly reduced power – who was rolled up in a carpet and trampled to death by horses. In an orgy of destruction, centuries of Muslim intellectual and literary treasures were burnt or thrown into the river Tigris. The time of Iraq as a centre of power and culture was finally over, and Cairo would now become the hub of the Islamic world until 1453, when Christian Constantinople would fall to the Turks.

Miraculously, the West was once again saved from seemingly certain destruction when the Great Khan Mongke died invading a Chinese province in 1259, and Hulegu was forced to return home to take part in the leadership struggle. What remained of his forces in the west was decisively beaten by the Mamluks.

Kublai Khan (AD 1215–1294)

The Mongol leader chosen to succeed Mongke was Kublai Khan. While in theory, he ruled the largest land empire in history, by this time the Mongolian Empire had been bequeathed to Genghis' four sons in the form of four territories. These had become de facto independent empires, or 'khanates', each ruled by a separate khan and pursuing its own distinct interests and objectives.

The greatest khanate – that of Mongolia, Korea, Tibet and parts of China – was ruled by Kublai, who completed the subjugation of China, effectively ending the rule of the Sung Dynasty. The second khanate, the Chagatai Khanate, comprised much of Central Asia, whilst the third – known as the Il-Khanate, and created by Hulegu – ruled over Persia and the Middle East.[42] The fourth, and longest-lasting, was the Kipchak Khanate, or 'Golden Horde', which eventually included most of Russia, Poland and Hungary.

Kublai Khan relocated the imperial capital of the Mongolian Empire from Karakorum, in Mongolia, to Beijing, in northern China. Having conquered all of southern China, Kublai Khan added Emperor of China to his long list of titles, even adopting a Chinese dynastic name – the Yuan. This dynasty enjoyed a century-long reign in China.

Wishing to extend his lands further, in 1274 and 1281 Kublai Khan launched two major assaults on Japan, both of which were hindered by terrible storms. The Japanese believed the winds had been sent by the gods to protect them, calling them 'divine wind', or *kamikaze*.

Outside China, the other khanates had slowly started to pay less attention to the demands of the Great Khan and begun to govern themselves, in part because they felt the Great Khanate in the east had forsaken its Mongolian roots and become too Chinese. These initial fractures had only been exacerbated by the struggles for succession following the death of Great Khan Mongke in around 1260. The death-knell of the unified

---

[42]   The Chagatai Khanate grew steadily until the rise of Tamerlane, who destroyed its power. After Tamerlane's death, the Khanate remained as a minor state until the Qing Dynasty of China annexed it in the 18th century. The Il-Khanate of Persia, founded by Hulegu in 1260, survived for only a short time and collapsed into various successor states, with its Mongol ruling class eventually embracing Islam and being absorbed into the native populations of Persia and Iraq.

Mongol empire had been sounded, and Kublai Khan was the last to hold the title of Great Khan of the Mongols.

The Ascent of Moscow

In Russia, the Mongols of the Golden Horde ruled Kievan Rus through local princes who paid tribute to them. By assisting the Mongols in collecting these tributes, the insignificant trading outpost of Moscow began to flourish around the turn of the 14th century, becoming a relatively safe place to live and attracting more wealth and people as a result. The city's importance was put beyond doubt when the Patriarchate of the Russian Orthodox Church transferred there from the town of Vladimir, making it the spiritual capital of Russia.

By 1480 the grand princes of Muscovy had accumulated so much wealth that nobody could challenge them. Grand Duke Ivan III of Muscovy – father of Ivan IV, known as 'the Terrible' – began subjugating Moscow's rival cities, and became the first Muscovite leader to adopt the title of tsar and 'Ruler of all Rus'. It was during his reign that northern Russia was united under one sovereign, shaking off the yoke of Mongol rule.

Although Mongol rule allowed Muscovy to grow and develop at the expense of the surrounding city states, effectively fuelling the expansion of the nascent Russian Empire, it also isolated Russia from Europe. This partly explains why the kinds of major social and political reforms that were being introduced in Europe in the wake of the Renaissance and the Reformation did not reach Russia. Europe developed a middle class; Russia did not. This was to have profound consequences for the country's subsequent development.

The Legacy of the Mongols

In terms of territory, the Mongols were the greatest conquerors of all time, bringing almost the entire continent of Asia under the control of one Great Khan; only the British Empire in the 19th century had a larger dominion, albeit more geographically disparate. Unlike the Confucian Chinese, who considered traders parasites, the Mongols fortunately recognised the importance of commerce. By improving communications within their empire, and by permitting European merchants to journey overland as far as China for the first time, the Mongols effectively put the East in touch with the West. Trade routes were reopened that had lain dormant since the time of Muhammad.

It was during this period that Marco Polo came to the Mongolian empire. This 13th century explorer from Venice spent many years at the court of Kublai Khan and travelled throughout his domain. Later, imprisoned during a war between Venice and Genoa, he dictated a book recounting his time in Mongolia, which became famous in Europe.

As we will see, it was contact with the East – and the ensuing insatiable European demand for its silk and spices – that encouraged Europeans to seek a western sea route to Asia, thereby 'discovering' America in the process.

The Hundred Years War in Europe (AD 1337–1453)

In Europe, meanwhile, 1337 saw England go to war with France over the inheritance of the French crown. This strife would rage on and off for a century – the longest single conflict in English history. French support for the Scots in the face of English intervention in Scotland only inflamed tensions further. Thanks to the superiority of their archers, the English won a series of major battles over the coming century – the battles of Crecy in 1346 and Agincourt in 1415 are just two of the better-known examples – in which the flower of French aristocracy was destroyed.

By the 1420s, England possessed most of present-day France north of the Loire River, and France appeared to have been decisively beaten. However, the sheer length of the war, and the burden of taxation which was required to finance it,[43] had worn the English down. Ultimately, they found themselves unable to withstand the force of a united France under Joan of Arc, and they were driven from French soil. The capture of Bordeaux by the French in 1453, just as Constantinople was falling to the Ottomans, marked the end of the war. Before fleeing, however, the English managed to seize Joan of Arc, trying her for heresy and burning her at the stake.

Ten years into the Hundred Years War, Europe had been hit by a devastating plague brought in on ships from Asia, where it had originated in the 1330s. Called the 'Black Death' after the blackening of skin around its symptomatic swellings, the plague wiped out some 20 million people – between one quarter and one third of Europe's population – between 1347 and 1351.

The largely uneducated non-Jewish European populations noted the lower incidence of the disease among religious groups who prescribed ritual washing, such as Jews and Muslims. As a result, many blamed the Jews for the plague, or accused them of sorcery, often murdering them or driving them from towns. In a frenzy of religious hatred, Jews would eventually be expelled from France in 1394, and Spain in 1492, having already been expelled from England in 1290.

---

[43]   These taxes were a key cause of The Peasants Revolt in England in 1381.

Both the plague and continuous warfare of the 14th century led people to question authority. The Church was not immune to this, and would shortly experience upheaval of its own which would further erode its power. In a dispute over the validity of a papal election in 1378, Europe was split between supporting an Italian pope in Rome and a French pope in Avignon in France, each of whom had excommunicated the other. This impasse lasted for 40 years, with each pope naming his own successor, and became known as the Great Western Schism. In an attempt to resolve the split, a third rival pope was proposed, although all three were eventually deposed in favour of a new pontiff, Martin V. His election, in 1417, restored stability, in the form of a single pope based in Rome, to the Catholic world. However, the schism had diminished the papacy and further decreased loyalty to the Church.[44]

The Rise of the Ottomans (c. AD 1300)

Weakened by civil war, and under constant pressure from the crusaders from the west, the Arabs from the south and the Mongols from the east, it was amazing that the Seljuk Sultanate lasted as long as it did. When it eventually disintegrated, the small remaining principalities all vied for supremacy. With the advent of peace – brought by the retreat of both the Mongols and the crusaders – one of these rose to dominance, and succeeded in building a powerful and extensive empire which endured for several hundred years: that of the Ottomans.

In 1301, the leader of this principality, Osman, defeated a Byzantine army a few miles from Constantinople. The prestige

---

[44] During the same Council, those gathered took the opportunity to try the Czech priest, Jan Hus (circa 1369-1415), for heresy. His crime was to complain about corruption in the Church and suggest that the Bible, rather than Church leaders, was the ultimate source of authority for Christians.

this conferred allowed him to consolidate Ottoman authority over a substantial area in north-western Anatolia (Turkey). The Ottomans expanded rapidly, absorbing weaker tribes to the east, and reducing the weakened Byzantine Empire to just the city of Constantinople by 1351. The Byzantine Emperor attempted to persuade the pope in Rome that, despite their differences, they had a common enemy. In the hope of receiving aid, in 1369 he even travelled to Rome in person to make public submission to the pope, but with no success.

In 1389, the Ottoman leader Murad I wiped out a huge combined army of Serbs, Albanians and Poles at the Battle of Kosovo Polje in present-day Serbia – another defining moment for the West. Shortly after the battle, the whole of Macedonia was incorporated into the Ottoman state. Murad himself was killed in the battle, but his son Bayezid succeeded him, and would eventually lay siege to Constantinople in 1394. It seemed that nothing could stop the Ottoman advance, and that the long-awaited collapse of the Byzantine Empire was finally at hand. However, at the last hour, it was the Ottoman Turks themselves who were attacked from the east. The capture of Constantinople would have to wait.

Tamerlane (AD 1336–1405)

The Mongol leader, Timur – or Tamerlane as he is referred to in the West – unwittingly came to the defence of Europe at the turn of the 15th century. Tamerlane had grown in power in the mid-14th century by taking advantage of the slow disintegration of the Chagatai Khanate, which had suffered a series of weak leaders. He was determined to make himself master of Central Asia. 'As there is but one God in heaven,' he said, 'there ought to be but one ruler on earth.' In an eight-year rampage (between 1396 and 1404) he conquered most of Central Asia, invaded northern India – executing up to 100,000 Indian prisoners in cold blood before the gates of Delhi – and destroyed Baghdad, slaughtering up to 20,000 of its inhabitants and making towers of their skulls. He also captured Syria, conquered Persia and received submission from Egypt.

Tamerlane's campaign in the west was directed against two enemies: the Ottomans and the Mamluks. After conquering the Mamluks, he successfully defeated an Ottoman army at the Battle of Ankara in 1402, capturing Sultan Bayezid in the process. The Sultan died in captivity, but only after having been paraded around in a cage – an ignominious end if ever there were one. The capture of the Sultan was greeted with rejoicing by the kings in the West, who even sent sycophantic messages to Tamerlane, hoping that he would ally with them against the Turks. Yet before any of his plans could be realised he died in 1405, at the age of 69, and his Timurid Empire didn't long outlive him. His legacy did continue in India, however, where his great-great-grandson Babur founded the Mughal Empire.

The Fall of Constantinople (AD 1453)
Bayezid's sons fought over their father's inheritance for the following ten years, until Mehmed I emerged as the new leader. He almost immediately went on the warpath, retaking most of the lands that Tamerlane had won from his father, while his son, Murad II, successfully defeated an alliance of Europeans responding to his invasion of Serbia in 1439.

It was Murad's son, Mehmed II, who finally brought an end to what was left of the Eastern Roman Empire[45], with a fifty-four-day siege of Constantinople. The walls that had defended

---

[45]   The last Byzantine emperor died in the siege.

Constantinople for centuries were finally brought down by a relatively new weapon – the cannon. One of Mehmed's first actions was to go to the Hagia Sophia – the great cathedral of Orthodox Christianity, built under Justinian – and, after a quick prayer of thanksgiving, ordered it to be turned into a mosque.

By the end of the 14th century, the Byzantine Empire's influence was long defunct and it no longer posed a military threat, consisting only of Constantinople and some surrounding land. The city itself had never really regained its grandeur following the crusader occupation of 1204-1261. Nevertheless, having been one of the greatest cities in the world for over 800 years, it is not difficult to imagine the sensation and terror that its fall would have caused in the West. It was, after all, still the capital of the Roman Empire, no matter how run-down. The fear that the Turks were about to overrun the entire continent even prompted Pope Pius II into offering to make Mehmed emperor if he converted to Christianity.

By this point, the Ottoman Sultan ruled over all the lands of Muslim Asia, extending to the Euphrates River in the east, and claimed superiority over all other Islamic rulers.[46] Constantinople became the new imperial capital, and gradually acquired the name of Istanbul.

In the West the war continued on both land and sea. Serbia capitulated shortly after the fall of Constantinople, and most of the Balkans followed thereafter. The Ottomans then overran the southernmost part of Greece, defeated Venice and landed on the heel of Italy. It was only the death of Mehmed II in 1481 that stopped the Ottoman troops from making further inroads into Europe, when they were ordered home to help the

---

[46]   The Ottoman Sultans would hold the title of Caliph until 1924.

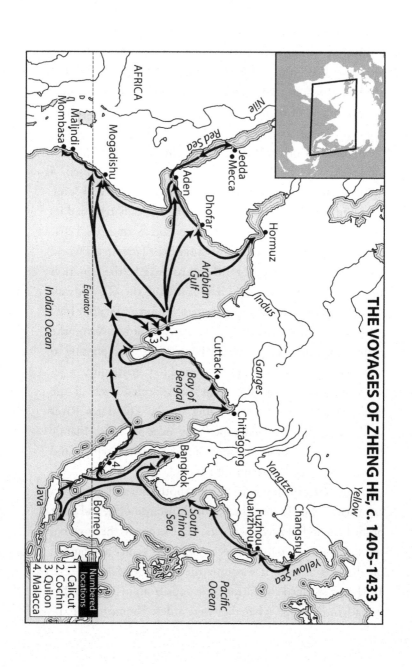

THE VOYAGES OF ZHENG HE, c. 1405–1433

AFRICA

Nile

Red Sea

Jedda
Mecca

Aden

Dhofar

Hormuz

Arabian
Gulf

Indus

Mogadishu

Majindi
Mombasa

Equator

Indian Ocean

Cuttack

Ganges

Bay of
Bengal

Chittagong

Bangkok

Borneo

South
China
Sea

Java

Yangtze

Fuzhou
Quanzhou

Changshu

Yellow

Yellow Sea

Pacific
Ocean

Numbered
locations
1. Calicut
2. Cochin
3. Quilon
4. Malacca

new Sultan defeat his brother in a leadership battle. Yet again, remarkably, Europe was saved at the eleventh hour.

Ming China (AD 1368–1644)

While the Ottomans were in the ascendancy in the Middle East, China missed its opportunity to become the major global power. The Chinese had never accepted their Mongolian Yuan overlords, whose treatment of them had led to growing discontent; the people had been taxed heavily to pay for expensive projects, including the building of roads and many ultimately unsuccessful military campaigns. Widespread crop failure in the north, resulting in famine in the 1340s, only served to break the back of an already overburdened system.

Hungry and homeless, the peasants united and rebelled. In the 1360s, one such peasant, a former Buddhist monk called Zhu Yuanzhang, was successful in extending his power throughout the Yangtze Valley. He seized Beijing in 1368, forced the Mongols to withdraw to Mongolia, took the title Hongwu, and declared himself the founder of a new Chinese ruling house: the Ming Dynasty.[47]

These new rulers were initially open to the world and encouraged trade. Under the reign of the second Ming emperor, the Chinese even embarked on a series of major naval expeditions. Between 1405 and 1433, many decades before Columbus or Magellan, several voyages of exploration and diplomacy were undertaken under the leadership of Admiral Zheng He, travelling around the Indian Ocean as far as Africa. These expeditions are said to have included up to 28,000 men on ships up to 300 feet long.

---

[47] 'Ming' means 'bright' or 'brilliant' in Chinese.

China's potential at this time seemed almost limitless; had they continued to look outwards, it might have been they who discovered America, rather than the Europeans.[48] Unfortunately for China, however, this was not to be. With the Mongols expelled, Confucian ministers gained power at the court of the Emperor. These ministers were hostile to both commerce and – perhaps understandably, following the recent Mongol occupation – all things foreign. They also had an unhealthy veneration for the past. 'Preserving the glories of the past seemed more important in China than addressing the kind of questions that global expansion was forcing onto Westerners' attention.'[49]

There were, to be sure, pressing domestic issues to deal with, not least the constant quest for resources with which to repel continuous and aggressive Mongol raids on their borders. Developing maritime trade was simply not a high priority.

Under the influence of Confucian ministers, the government ended its sponsorship of naval expeditions, dismantled shipyards and forbade the construction of multi-masted ships. Zheng He's records were destroyed in the 1470s, and by 1525 it was an offence to build any oceangoing vessel.[50] So ended the great age of Chinese exploration, and the development of world maritime trade was left to the Europeans, who were just beginning to embark on their voyages of discovery.

Without doubt, this was very much to the detriment of the country's subsequent development. Up until this time,

---

[48]   There are unproven theories that the Chinese did actually make it to America.

[49]   *Why the West Rules for Now* by Ian Morris, Profile Books.

[50]   China also took several steps backwards in other areas, even abolishing mechanical clocks after leading the world in clock construction.

China had been one of the most technologically advanced countries in the world, inventing, amongst other things, paper, gunpowder, porcelain and the magnetic compass. However, with so much power residing in the person of the emperor, a single imperial decision could – and often did – halt innovation while the country's fervent veneration for tradition eventually became the enemy of invention. This was a profound disadvantage in a world where new ideas gave countries a competitive edge. Families tended 'to preserve what was ancient and hallowed at the expense of what was new but potentially disruptive'.[51] Moreover, China's relative isolation from other countries only encouraged it to look inwards. Perhaps no greater example of this exists than the construction of the Great Wall of China, which was expressly built to keep foreigners out.

On the other hand, the fierce competition between Europe's collection of small, culturally and linguistically diverse states served as a distinct advantage to its inventors and explorers: if sponsorship from one party was not forthcoming, they could always turn to another. After all, it was in each country's best interest to keep up with the latest technologies in order to maintain the balance of power, and invention flourished as a result.

In the end, 'it was precisely the instability which Europeans had been trying unsuccessfully to evade for so long which had turned out to be their greatest strength. Their wars, their incessant internal struggles, their religious quarrels, all these had been the unfortunate but necessary condition of the intellectual growth which had led them, unlike their Asiatic neighbours, to develop the metaphysical and inquiring

---

[51] *Worlds at War* by Anthony Pagden, Oxford Edition.

attitudes towards nature which, in turn, had given them the power to transform and control the worlds in which they lived.'[52]

The Retreat of Islam

China was not the only civilisation to retreat into itself. Much of the Islamic world, formerly a beacon of progress in a backward world, became seemingly trapped by the limits of scripture, unprepared to accept the value of any teaching or development not expressly mentioned in the Qur'an. As David Landes states: 'Islamic science, denounced as heresy by religious zealots, bent under theological pressure for spiritual conformity.'[53]

Resistance to the idea of a printed Qur'an extended to all use of the printing press in many Islamic countries, whereas it became the prime conduit for the spreading of ideas during the Renaissance, leading to the intellectual development of Western Europe. What nobody could have predicted was the extent and speed at which Europe would ultimately grow.

---

[52]   *Worlds at War* by Anthony Pagden, Oxford Edition.

[53]   *The Wealth and Poverty of Nations* by David Landes, Abacus.

V

THE ASCENT OF THE WEST

(AD 1450 – 1800)

It was fortuitous for Europe that both China and the Islamic world were simultaneously turning their backs on progress. Having, until that point, lagged behind them both in its general development, it was about to witness a shift that would drag it out of the Middle Ages, change the course of history, and lead to European domination of the world.

The Renaissance (early 15th – late 16th Centuries)

The causes of this shift were manifold: the increased exchange of ideas and goods following the end of the Crusades; the discovery of new worlds, which led people to question their beliefs; challenges to both the teachings and authority of the Church following repeated schisms; and the sudden influx into Europe of knowledge brought by scholars fleeing the Ottoman advance.

Often referred to as the Renaissance – from the French word for 'rebirth' – the period which is generally agreed to have spanned the early 15th to the late 16th centuries saw a deep transformation in the way Europeans thought, ruled and lived.

The most important technical and cultural innovation of the Renaissance was the introduction of Gutenberg's printing press, around 1450. Without the ability to spread new ideas rapidly and cheaply, the remarkable speed with which Europe developed would have been most unlikely. The printing press saw the start of a communications revolution in which, by 1480, books were being printed in the major cities of Germany, France, the Netherlands, England and Poland. To put this into perspective: 'in the 50 years following the invention more books were produced than in the preceding thousand years.'[54] With larger print runs came lower unit costs, both improving the availability of books and making them cheaper for the wider public. That books were also increasingly published in the vernacular – the local language of a region – rather than Latin may well have helped reinforce a sense of national identity.

While the printing press powered the Renaissance, the effects of its invention might not have been so dramatic had Europe not been experiencing a period of relative peace. The Hundred Years War between France and England had ended in 1453, and Christian armies had finally evicted the Muslims from what is now Spain[55]. Trade and agriculture, so long disrupted – first by the Barbarian invasions of the 4th and 5th centuries, then by the hostility between Christianity and Islam – flourished again, and feudalistic European society was slowly replaced by a trade-centred one.

The Italians – the Florentines and Venetians in particular – exploited their location between East and West to accumulate

---

[54] *The Lever of Riches* by Joel Mokyr, Oxford University Press.

[55] In the early 15th century, five independent kingdoms occupied the Iberian Peninsula: Portugal, Navarre, Castile, Aragon, and the last Muslim stronghold of Granada. In 1469, the Crown of Castile was united with the Crown of Aragon through the marriage of Isabella, heiress of Castile, to Ferdinand, heir to the throne of Aragon. In 1492, this 'Union of the Crowns' succeeded in expelling the remaining Muslims from Granada and, when the Kingdom of Navarre was annexed by the Union in 1512, modern Spain was established.

huge wealth. A life in business and politics became as respectable as a life in the Church. Many classical ideas, which had flown eastward with the fall of Rome a thousand years earlier, returned to Europe, leading to a revival in the intellectual and artistic appreciation of Greco-Roman culture. Non-religious themes were no longer frowned upon, and rich patrons funded the construction of buildings of a scale and grandeur unseen since Roman times. Great families such as the Medici became renowned as patrons of the arts, whose flourishing defines the Renaissance for many; Leonardo da Vinci and Michelangelo are just two of the brightest stars in a constellation of artists who reaped the benefits of such patronage during this time. Tremendous advances were also made in the fields of mathematics, medicine, engineering and architecture.

The Age of Exploration (1450-1600)

The capture of Constantinople by the Ottoman Turks in 1453 acted as a key driver for European exploration. Overland journeys into Persia, Central Asia and China were lengthy and dangerous, and required the expensive services of numerous middlemen. They were now taxed even further.

Long since addicted to silk and spices, and envying the riches of cities such as Venice, which had benefited from this trade, the Portuguese sought to develop a sea route around Africa to reach the East. In this way, they hoped to both bypass Ottoman taxes and undercut Italian trade.

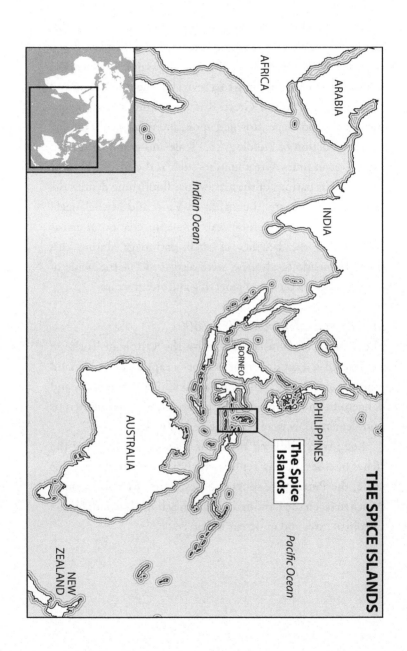

THE SPICE ISLANDS

The Spice Islands

AFRICA

ARABIA

INDIA

Indian Ocean

BORNEO

PHILIPPINES

AUSTRALIA

Pacific Ocean

NEW
ZEALAND

The Spice Trade

Europeans had been trading with the East for centuries, generally through Arab and Indian intermediaries, selling bulk goods such as timber, glassware, soap, paper, copper and salt in return for silk, incense and spices. Silk was a luxury compared to the coarse cloth available at the time; incense was used to mask the smells of an unhygienic society; and spices (cloves, cinnamon, nutmeg and black pepper) were used to make food taste better, to preserve it and to hide the smell of spoiled meat. Lack of animal feed through the winter months meant that they were routinely slaughtered in autumn; with no ice available, the use of pepper – which has antibacterial properties – was one way in which meat could be preserved, although still far more expensive than salt.

Cloves were specifically prized by Europeans for their medicinal properties, but some doctors suggested that nutmeg could protect against the plague, with the result that, at one point, it became worth more than its weight in gold, causing people to risk their lives to import it. Pepper grew predominantly in India, whilst nutmeg and cloves could only be found in one place: a few small islands called the Moluccas (in present-day Indonesia), north-west of Papua New Guinea. These islands became known as the Spice Islands, and European attempts to find a westerly route to them would fundamentally affect the future of the world.

The other impetus to exploration was the need for gold. The Portuguese required the precious metal to pay for their imports from the East, but the main European access to it came from Africa via the trans-Sahara caravan routes. Several African kingdoms, such as Ghana, had grown fabulously wealthy on the back of this trade, and the Portuguese wanted to establish sea routes down the coast of the continent to obtain the gold at its source.

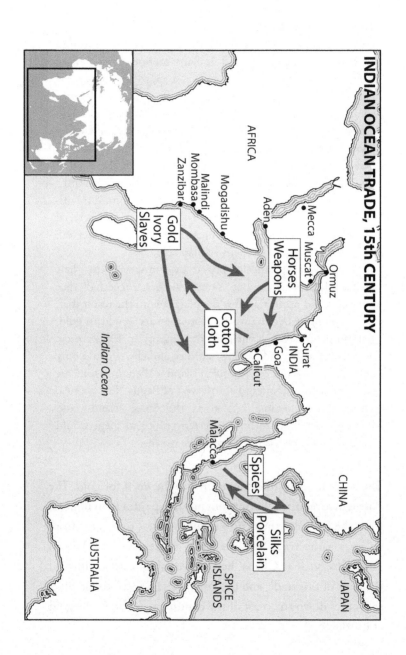

Working their way down the African coast, they rapidly proved that such small expeditions could be both successful and profitable. The son of the king of Portugal – Prince Henry, also known as 'the Navigator' – dreamt of establishing an ocean route to the Spice Islands, and consequently became a famous patron of the maritime sciences. In addition to funding voyages of discovery, he founded a school of seamanship in southern Portugal, where mapmakers, geographers, astronomers and navigators could discuss and improve upon the latest maritime technology.

One of the developments stemming from this initiative was the design of the caravel: a new type of ship that could travel faster and carry larger cargoes. Thanks to the shape and arrangement of its sails, it was better able to catch the wind and thus keep a straighter course, rather than having to zigzag constantly. This saved considerable journey time, and the new design came to play a major part in the 15th century voyages of discovery. Indeed, two of the three boats used by Christopher Columbus were caravels.

Prince Henry died in 1460, but his son, King João, maintained his patronage, and in 1486 sent Bartolemeu Dias to lead an expedition around the southern tip of Africa. Amongst other goals, Dias was ordered to try to make contact with the legendary Christian African king, Prester John, and request his help in overcoming Muslim dominance of the Indian Ocean trade. Prester John was never found, of course, as he never existed, but Dias returned to Lisbon 16 months later having successfully completed the first part of his mission. Dias named the tip of Africa *Cabo das Tormentas*, or 'Cape of Storms', in memory of the tempests he had experienced. The name was changed – allegedly by the king – to *Cabo da Boa*

Esperança, or the 'Cape of Good Hope', as he was hopeful, but not sure, that Dias had found a way to the East.

By rounding the Cape of Good Hope, Dias proved that the Atlantic and Indian Oceans were not landlocked, as many European geographers of the time believed, and showed that a sea route to India might indeed be feasible. This was big news indeed, and greatly encouraged those who looked for such a route to the East. However, before a further voyage could take place, some momentous news came from the court of the king and queen of Spain: an Italian sailor they had sponsored had supposedly found a route to the Orient by sailing west across the Atlantic. We now know that he had discovered the Americas.

Christopher Columbus (AD 1451–1506)

Christopher Columbus had been born in the Italian seaport of Genoa, but moved to Portugal in his twenties, where he helped his brother with his map-making business. Engrossed by the adventures of Marco Polo, it was here that he began to develop the idea not only that the Far East might be reached by sailing west, but also that this journey could be even shorter than the overland trade route.

The courts of Portugal, France and England all refused to sponsor his trip. The rounding of the Cape of Good Hope by Dias may have made Portugal consider the quest for a western route unnecessary. Help from England and France was simply not forthcoming. After expending considerable effort to raise the sponsorship he needed, he was introduced to King Ferdinand and Queen Isabella of the newly unified Spain. Both were greatly occupied by the final throes of the *Reconquista*, or 're-conquest': the long, expensive task of trying to win back the Iberian Peninsula from the Moors – Columbus informed them that a westerly route would allow Spain entry into the lucrative spice trade, hitherto monopolised by the Italians, and bring them great riches.

Sensing victory over the Moors, and eventually realising the scale of the opportunity presented by Columbus, Ferdinand and Isabella provided him with the resources he needed to undertake the voyage. And so, in August 1492, Columbus set sail from Spain with three ships and a crew of 90. Massively misjudging the size of the globe – due in part to an overestimation of Asia's size by map makers, following the publication of Marco Polo's writings – it took two whole months before land was sighted. The first glimpse was of one of the islands now known as the Bahamas. Columbus called it San Salvador, in recognition of a safe crossing, and called the natives Indians, believing he had reached the Indies. In a further misapprehension, he mistook Cuba for Japan, or possibly even China.

Returning to Spain with small traces of gold, a few 'Indians' and some parrots to prove that he had found land, Columbus was paid handsomely, and appointed Admiral of the Seas and Viceroy and Governor of the Indies – titles he had requested upon his departure. News of the discovery spread rapidly thanks to the printing press, and contributed greatly to the Renaissance spirit of questioning long-held assumptions about the world.

Columbus returned three more times to America. During the second voyage, between 1493 and 1496, a settlement was founded, with Columbus serving as its governor. It became Santo Domingo, capital of the present-day Dominican Republic. Yet his inadequacy as an administrator was such that, when he returned there on his third trip in 1498, he needed to ask Spain for assistance in governing the settlement. Instead of

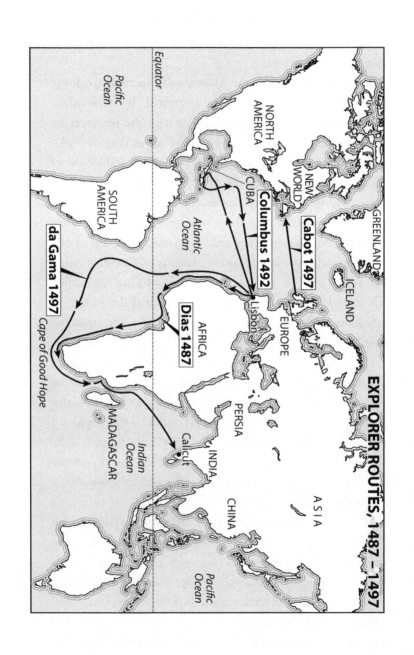

EXPLORER ROUTES, 1487 – 1497

Equator

Pacific
Ocean

NORTH
AMERICA

NEW
WORLD

GREENLAND

ICELAND

SOUTH
AMERICA

Atlantic
Ocean

CUBA

Columbus 1492

Cabot 1497

Lisbon

EUROPE

da Gama 1497

Dias 1487

AFRICA

PERSIA

ASIA

CHINA

Cape of Good Hope

MADAGASCAR

Indian
Ocean

Calicut

INDIA

Pacific
Ocean

sending help, they dispatched a new governor who promptly arrested Columbus, along with his two brothers, returning him to Spain in chains. When he was finally released, Queen Isabella agreed to fund his fourth voyage.

When Columbus died in 1506, he still believed that he had reached Asia. What's more, although his fourth voyage saw him land on the South American mainland, he never set foot on the North American mainland. This was the privilege of Giovanni Caboto (John Cabot) – an Italian working under the patronage of King Henry VII of England – in 1497. However, even Caboto initially believed he had landed in Asia.

It was an Italian named Amerigo Vespucci, who undertook voyages between 1499 and 1502 on behalf of Spain and Portugal, who established beyond doubt that Columbus had reached a new continent, and it was the feminised Latin form of his name[56] that marked it on a new map of the world in 1507. Only then did the first recognisable modern image of the planet begin to emerge; up until that point, the extent of people's geographical knowledge was limited to that of the ancient Greeks.

Why was it the Westerners who sought a path to the East in the age of exploration, rather than the Easterners who sought a path to the West? One of the answers with regard to the Chinese was that their ministers distrusted change after centuries of war against foreign invaders. Moreover, Easterners had comparatively little incentive to go either east or west; the West had few innovations of interest and little to offer aside from less-advanced minor kingdoms, while the seemingly empty Pacific was hardly enticing with so much trade already existing in the Indian Ocean. They missed their opportunity.

---

56   The names of continents are traditionally feminine.

In the West, an exploration race began as soon as Columbus returned from his first voyage, with Portuguese efforts increasingly focused on establishing a maritime route to the East. Vasco da Gama was appointed to lead an expedition to complete the voyage to India begun by Dias ten years earlier.

With the help of Arab navigators whom he picked up on the east coast of Africa, da Gama landed at Calicut on the Indian coast in 1498. Despite an extremely difficult and lengthy return journey in which over half his crew died from hunger, scurvy and other diseases, he returned, bearing spices, to a hero's welcome in Lisbon. By this time, he had been away for more than two years and had crossed more than 24,000 miles of open sea. Da Gama was famous: he had discovered a sea route to India. It seemed unlikely that Spain could cap such an achievement.

Shortly after da Gama's return, a second voyage, involving more ships and over 1,000 men, was dispatched, this time under the leadership of Pedro Cabral. Dias also took part in this journey, but perished – perhaps appropriately, given his previous experience there – in a storm off the Cape of Good Hope. Cabral's journey saw the initiation of a brutal European takeover of the Spice Islands. Unsettled by the thought of losing their trade to Europeans, some Muslim merchants opened fire on Cabral's men, a number of whom were killed. Cabral took bloody revenge, killing several hundred Muslims in retaliation. Da Gama, who followed with another expedition the following year, did not act any more nobly, robbing and murdering wherever and whenever he deemed it necessary. As a consequence, the people of the East Indies nursed a deep hatred for da Gama and, by association, the Portuguese. When, a few years later, they welcomed the Dutch with open

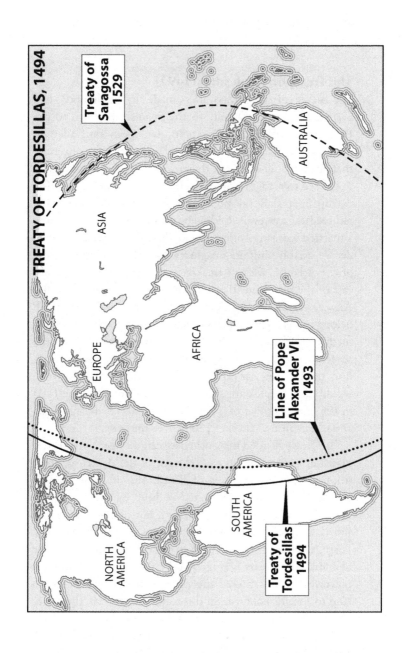

TREATY OF TORDESILLAS, 1494

Treaty of
Saragossa
1529

AUSTRALIA

ASIA

EUROPE

AFRICA

Line of Pope
Alexander VI
1493

NORTH
AMERICA

SOUTH
AMERICA

Treaty of
Tordesillas
1494

arms, little did they suspect that they would be equally, if not more, brutal.

The Treaty of Tordesillas (1494)

The news of the discoveries made by Columbus had been momentous not only to the Spanish, but also to the Portuguese, who until that point had been unrivalled in maritime exploration. They immediately became concerned that Spain would challenge their own future territorial claims, so refused to recognise Spanish claims to these new lands. The corrupt Spanish Borgia pope, Alexander VI – who incidentally fathered at least seven children by various mistresses including a married woman – offered to mediate. In 1493, he issued a decree establishing an imaginary line through the middle of the Atlantic, west of the coast of north-west Africa, and east of the new lands that Columbus had claimed for Spain. Any newly discovered lands to the east would henceforth belong to Portugal, and those to the west to Spain. Following further exploration, the Portuguese grew dissatisfied with the agreement, claiming that their ships needed to travel further into the Atlantic to exploit those favourable winds which would carry them south and east. Consequently, in June 1494 in the Spanish town of Tordesillas the line was renegotiated and re-established another 1300 km to the west.

The Treaty divided the world between the age's two greatest maritime powers. Spain gained most of the Americas, apart from the easternmost area of Brazil. This was allocated to Portugal once it was discovered in 1500 by the Portuguese sailor, Pedro Cabral, and explains why Portuguese is spoken in Brazil, whereas Spanish dominates the rest of South America. Portugal retained control of the potentially navigable sea route to India. The Treaty was ignored by the northern European powers, who questioned the right of the pope to allocate land to specific countries in this way. Nevertheless, the treaty effectively gave Spain a new empire, and this would have profound consequences for the unfolding history of Europe and the Americas.

The short-term effect of Da Gama's remarkable discovery of the long-sought-after sea-route to India was spectacular: it changed the balance of power in Europe. In the West, Venice and northern Italy lost their monopoly on trade with the Orient: a loss from which they would never recover. The Italians sponsored their own seagoing expeditions, but evidently with little success. In the East, meanwhile, the importance of overland trade routes of the Arabs and Turks diminished, contributing to the slow but inexorable decline of the Ottoman Empire.

Ferdinand Magellan (1480–1521)

The Spanish, however, did not rest on their laurels. The young Charles I of Spain sponsored a westward expedition by Ferdinand Magellan, having been convinced by him that, according to the Treaty of Tordesillas, the Spice Islands rightly belonged to Spain, not Portugal. By 1507 it had become clear that America was not in fact Asia, and that the Indies actually lay beyond it through unnavigated waters. Numerous expeditions to find a way through had been dispatched in the early 16th century, all without success; if Magellan could find a route, Spain would become rich. With this in mind, an expedition under his leadership was sponsored by Charles I, and he set sail in 1519.

After a tempestuous voyage down the east coast of South America, in October 1520 a passage was spotted that led them to the calm waters of another ocean. Magellan named this *Mar Pacifico* as it was so peaceful compared to the Atlantic. He then set off to find the Spice Islands, but just as Columbus had underestimated the size of the Atlantic Ocean, so Magellan misjudged the Pacific, which is twice its size. It was another 14 weeks before they reached the small island of Guam. From here, they sailed on to the Philippines, only for Magellan to be killed after having become involved in a battle between local chieftains.

Only one ship from the fleet,[57] captained by Juan Sebastian del Cano, successfully returned to Spain in September 1522, having completed the first ever circumnavigation of the globe. The returning crew represented barely one tenth of the men who had embarked on the trip, although they bore with them 26 tonnes of cloves, which paid for the entire expedition. Whilst Del Cano achieved fame for this first circumnavigation, since Magellan had visited south-east Asia on a previous expedition, he is credited today with being the first man to go all the way around the world, albeit in two separate voyages. An epic tale of endurance, and one of the greatest adventures in the history of navigation, this voyage both revealed the true scale of our planet and proved that it was possible to sail around it.

The Spanish immediately claimed the Spice Islands. This was fiercely contested by the Portuguese, who paid them a huge quantity of gold to relinquish their claim after an amendment was made to the Treaty of Tordesillas. Portugal's domination of trade in the Indian Ocean was thus confirmed and, as compensation, Spain was given the rights to trade in the Philippines. The two countries dominated commerce in the area until other European powers succeeded in developing their navies and merchant fleets a century or so later.

Around this time, two things happened in Europe that were to have a huge and lasting impact on the history of Europe and, consequently, the world. First, in 1517, the German monk, Martin Luther, shocked by what he had seen

---

[57]   The rest were captured, burned or shipwrecked.

on a journey to Rome, publicly criticised the Roman Catholic Church, precipitating an unprecedented religious and social revolution. Second, in 1519, the deeply Catholic Charles I of Spain inherited the Habsburg lands, becoming Charles V, ruler of the largest western empire since Roman times.

The European Reformation (1517–1598)

Luther was not the first to challenge the teachings of the Church. Preachers such as the Englishman John Wycliffe and the Bohemian Jan Hus had already asserted that people had the right to read and interpret the Bible for themselves, becoming subject to church persecution as a result. The Church had increasingly abused its power during the previous centuries, regularly demanding money from its flock and growing rich on the proceeds, so when Europe's population became generally more urbanised and educated, they began to resent the clergy's unreasonable demands.

What had so scandalised Luther on his journey to Rome in 1510 was the sale of indulgences – documents issued by the Church which would supposedly reduce time spent in purgatory and grant the buyer remission from the need to do penance for sins. His reading of the Bible had led him to the conclusion that one did not need to labour to win God's favour, as God's behaviour could not be influenced in that way. Christians were, rather, saved by faith alone; no amount of good works, or even the purchase of indulgences, made any difference at all. As a consequence, Luther rejected the authority of the pope, denied that priests had any special power over laypeople and asserted that the Bible was the sole source of Christian truth. 'One did not need to do penance, to make costly pilgrimages, to venerate the wasted carcasses of supposed saints; one did not need to make sacrifices. Above all one did not need to buy the tawdry goods the Church peddled to its deluded flock in order to raise the cash it needed for its wars, for its vast buildings, for the paintings, the sculptures, the carved woodwork, the golden goblets and the bejewelled inlaid cases in which the relics of the sanctified laid, and that it relentlessly commissioned from all the finest and most expensive artists and craftsmen in Europe.'[58]

In 1517, as the Ottomans were capturing Egypt from the Mamluks – whose economy had also suffered from the discovery of the maritime spice route – Luther wrote his famous 95 arguments against the sale of indulgences and sent them to his local bishop. With the help of his friends and facilitated by the printing process, Luther's arguments spread like wildfire, leading Pope Leo X to condemn his teachings in a papal decree.

Not one to be told what to do, Luther burned this decree, as a result of which, in 1521, he was invited by Emperor Charles V to recant his views. With the Ottomans too close for comfort, Charles couldn't afford a divided Germany. Luther refused, insisting that he would only recant if the scriptures moved him to do so. For this, he was outlawed as a heretic. Fortunately for Luther, many German princes were keen to remain independent from the encroaching Spanish power, and he gained the protection of one of them.

Luther's challenging of traditions and ecclesiastical authority made him the focus for pent-up religious and economic discontent, with many peasants using the opportunity to air their resentment of Church authority. It seemed obvious to many of them that the Church favoured their oppressors. These complaints gained traction, turning

---

[58] *Worlds at War* by Anthony Pagden, Oxford Press.

into a rebellion, and then, in 1525, into a full-scale peasant revolt. Unfortunately for the peasants, Luther had not intended to incite a social revolution, merely a religious one, and gave his full support to the German nobles intent on putting out the flames of insurrection.

It was not long before the Reformation swept through Western Europe, fuelling long-standing international and dynastic disputes with a new religious dimension that seemed to preclude the possibility of compromise. '.[59] While Luther was most influential in Germany, the Swiss and the Dutch were heavily swayed by the Protestant teachings of an exile from France, John Calvin, who preached predestination – the idea that God had already decided who would be damned and who would be saved.[60] French adherents to the new teaching – known as Huguenots – were brutally suppressed, and war raged between Protestants and Catholics there until freedom of worship was finally granted in 1598 by Henry IV, under the Edict of Nantes.[61] In England, King Henry VIII had quickly exploited the teachings of Protestantism to renounce the authority of the pope completely, allowing him to divorce his Catholic wife – the daughter of Ferdinand and Isabella of Spain, Catherine of Aragon.

The Reformation had a huge impact, both positive and negative, on the development of the West. It allowed swathes of Europe to throw off the shackles of Catholic dogma and develop the freedom of thought that was necessary for innovation; but it also divided the Christians of northern

---

[59] *The Rise and Fall of the Great Powers* by Paul Kennedy. Reprinted with permission of HarperCollins Publishers © 1989 Paul Kennedy.

[60] Incidentally, the Lutherans and Calvinists came to despise each other.

[61] Not before half a million Protestants were expelled from France.

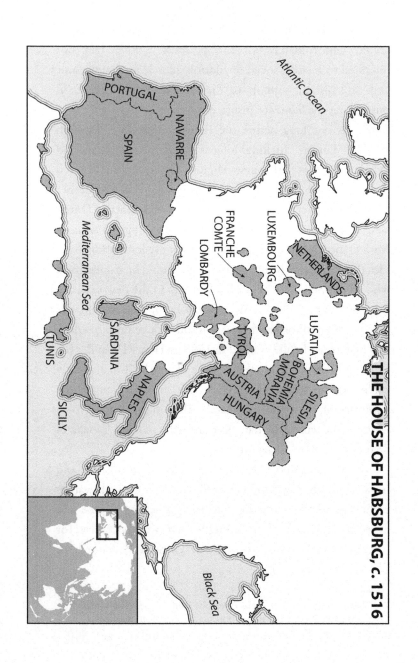

THE HOUSE OF HABSBURG, c. 1516

and southern Europe, ultimately leading to religious wars that would not abate until 1648.

The Habsburgs take over Europe

By the time Charles became Holy Roman Emperor in 1519, his Habsburg family, through numerous advantageous marriages, possessed the largest western empire since Roman times. This included Spain, the Netherlands, Austria and several smaller countries, not to mention Spain's rich, though unexplored, territories in the Americas. His empire encompassed so many cultures and languages that he was said to have spoken Spanish to God, French to his mistress, and German to his horse. King of Spain since 1516, he began to regard the country as the most important part of his empire, leaving the German-speaking provinces to be governed by his brother, Ferdinand.

Ruling as Emperor for 39 years during a period of tremendous European upheaval, Charles V spent his reign fighting against the French over lands in Italy and the Netherlands,[62] against a defensive league of Protestant princes in Germany and against the Ottoman Turks in the Mediterranean. He even fought the pope, sacking Rome in 1527 and driving the pontiff into exile in retaliation for the Vatican having allied itself with the French. Beyond Europe, Charles oversaw the Spanish colonisation of the Americas, including the conquest of both the Aztec and Inca empires.

---

[62] In which he surprisingly allied with Henry VIII of England.

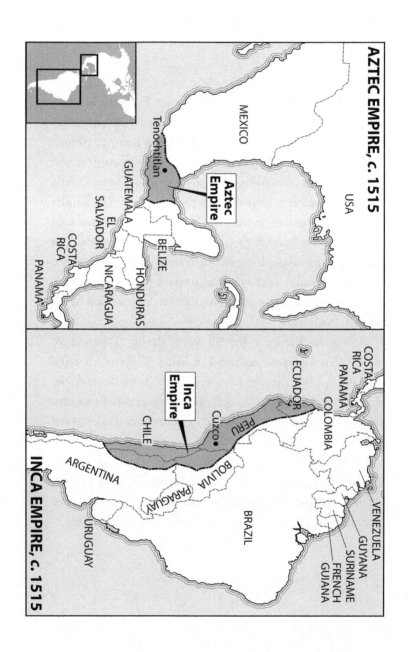

AZTEC EMPIRE, c. 1515

MEXICO

USA

Tenochtitlan

Aztec
Empire

GUATEMALA

BELIZE

EL
SALVADOR

HONDURAS

COSTA
RICA

NICARAGUA

PANAMA

INCA EMPIRE, c. 1515

COSTA
RICA

PANAMA

ECUADOR

COLOMBIA

Inca
Empire

Cuzco

PERU

CHILE

BOLIVIA

PARAGUAY

ARGENTINA

BRAZIL

URUGUAY

VENEZUELA

GUYANA

SURINAME

FRENCH
GUIANA

The Aztecs and the Incas meet the Iron Age
(1200–1520/1531)

Not long after the first Europeans landed in the Americas, rumours spread of kingdoms rich with gold. These tales proved to be true, and gold was indeed found in quantities beyond their wildest dreams. Columbus had sailed west to find a route to riches in the East, but his successors ended up finding much greater riches along the way.

Two major empires in the Americas were ruled by the Aztecs of present-day Mexico and the Incas, whose empire was possibly the largest in the world at the time, covering an area incorporating lands in present-day Ecuador, Chile, Peru, Argentina and Bolivia. Earlier civilisations in the area, such as the Olmecs and the Mayans, had expired for unknown reasons. By the time the conquistadors arrived in the early 16th century, the 300-year-old Aztec empire and that of the Incas were at their height.

The conquistadors' lust for gold led to their brutal overthrow of these empires. Hernan Cortes subjugated the Aztecs between 1519 and 1520, and Francisco Pizarro conquered the Incas a decade later. It is noteworthy that, in both cases relatively few Europeans were able to overcome vastly superior numbers.

It is possible that the Aztec emperor Montezuma, reigning from the large city of Tenochtitlan, may have mistaken Cortes for a returning god and lowered his guard. The Aztecs were also terrified by guns and horses, neither of which they had seen before; indeed, whilst early kinds of horses occupied the Americas until around 12,000 years ago, there is no record of modern horses being present there before the Europeans arrived in 1492. Additionally, Cortes found allies among local populations who had been subjugated by Aztec emperors.

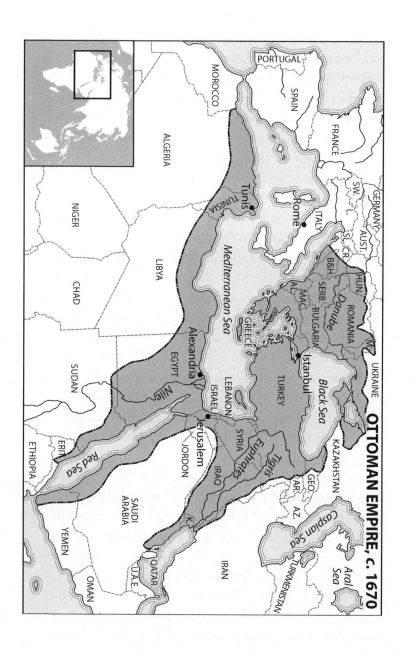

OTTOMAN EMPIRE, c. 1670

Finally, Cortes famously burned the ships in which his troops had travelled, forcing them to either fight or die.

Pizarro, on the other hand, captured the Incan king, Atahualpa, and held him for ransom until the Incas filled a large room – 22 feet long, 17 feet wide and 8 feet high – with gold. Pizarro then reneged on his promises and murdered the king, although not before baptising him, of course. According to various sources, the Spanish managed to defeat an Incan army of up to 80,000 soldiers with only 168 of their own. Previously unencountered European diseases killed huge numbers of the local population before the forces even joined in battle. When the indigenous people did successfully come together to defend themselves, 'the result was what one might expect from the clash between a Bronze Age culture and one of the most technologically advanced in Europe. Whilst their weaponry was by no means inefficient – the Aztecs' obsidian blades, in particular, were reputedly capable of decapitating a horse – it was no match for the combination of cavalry, crossbows and state-of-the-art firearms, blades and armour which the conquistadors had at their disposal.'

Back in Spain, meanwhile, Charles V encouraged the marriage of his son, Philip, to Mary Tudor, the Catholic queen of England, in order to link Spain, England and the Netherlands in a union of Catholic states. He was determined that Protestantism would not be permitted to gain a stronger foothold in Europe, afraid of the dissent it would encourage, and clearly saw little difference between Protestants and Turks. He missed the opportunity to put down the religious revolt in Germany, however, distracted as he was with wars against the French and the Ottomans, and with Luther himself under the protection of a group of German princes.

By the time he was ready to make a move, Protestantism was too deeply entrenched – at least in northern Germany – and, in 1555, at the Peace of Augsburg, Charles was forced to grant Lutheranism official status within the Holy Roman Empire. Much to his dismay, the treaty also allowed the 225 German princes to choose between Catholicism or Lutheranism as the official religion within their domains.

The Ottomans, for their part, remained a thorn in Charles' side, unsuccessfully attempting to take Vienna in 1529,[63] and remaining a powerful naval force in the Mediterranean until well after his death. Under Suleiman I – 'the Magnificent' – the Ottomans would continue to wage war against both the Habsburg Empire in the west and the Shiite Safavid Persians, with whom they shared a huge common frontier, in the east. Yet in the wake of a succession of incompetent Sultans, and with an increasingly repressive attitude to free thought, the over-extended Ottoman Empire would gradually decline from the 17th century onwards.

Safavid Persia (1502–1732)

In the confusion left by the retreating Mongols of Tamerlane, the Shiite Safavid dynasty had seized power in Persia. They established a strong independent state, although they were eventually forced to cede Baghdad and all of Iraq to the Ottoman Turks, whose interests were in conflict with their own. Shah Abbas (1571–1629) was the most renowned of the Safavid Shahs, but he was followed by weaker rulers, rendering Persia less of a threat to the Ottomans. A weak Persia would later become the focus of a struggle between the Russians and the British in the 19th century.

---

[63]   The Ottomans would try to capture Vienna again in 1683 and fail again.

The Catholic Counter-Reformation (1545)

Responding to the growth of the Protestant movement, the Catholic Church instituted its own reforms. In 1545 Pope Paul III convened the Council of Trent to reform the Church and to refute Lutheranism. However, a defensive measure, whereby the full fury of the Church could be unleashed on anybody challenging its authority, was also introduced. It was this Council that endorsed the establishment of the Roman Inquisition, which would hunt down and execute heretics in the most gruesome of ways. An index of books deemed heretical was published, in the first example of mass censorship. To read any of them was to run the risk of excommunication, which to many represented a fate worse than death.

In 1543 the Polish astronomer, Nicolai Copernicus, had been condemned for daring to suggest that the Earth, far from being the centre of the universe, actually rotated around the sun. 72 years later, Galileo Galilei was summoned to Rome by the Inquisition for having the audacity to agree with Copernicus. Whilst acknowledging that the Bible was infallible, he had had the temerity to suggest that those who interpreted it might not be. As a result, he was forced to state publicly that the Earth did not, in fact, revolve around the sun, and was sentenced to imprisonment in his own home. In short, 'the Protestant reformation gave a big boost to literacy, spawned dissent and heresies, and promoted scepticism and refusal of authority that is at the heart of the scientific endeavour. The Catholic countries, instead of meeting the challenge, responded by closure and censure.'[64]

Exhausted by wars on all fronts, Charles abdicated in 1555, only to die in a monastery two years later. The German-

---

[64]   *The Wealth and Poverty of Nations* by David Landes, Abacus.

speaking Habsburg lands passed to Charles' younger brother, Ferdinand, who became Holy Roman Emperor – now a virtually hereditary Habsburg title. The Spanish Empire – including the Netherlands – the Habsburg Italian possessions and, for a time, Portugal, passed to his fanatical son, Philip II. In this way, the minor branch of the Austrian Habsburgs and the major branch of the Spanish Habsburgs were founded.

The Dutch Revolt (1579–1648)

Philip II attempted to impose a more centralised system of government, partly to indulge his autocratic tendencies and partly to increase tax revenues to fund the spiralling costs of his wars. As a champion of Catholicism, Philip II was also intent on repressing Protestants – hitherto tolerated in the Netherlands in the interests of trade – wherever he found them.

The beginning of Philip II's reign saw simmering discontent among the Dutch, whose country had only formally been added to the possessions of Spain by Charles in 1549. Fiercely autonomous, they resented the new taxes levied by Philip II. A series of bad harvests provoked mass unrest, leading to the sacking of numerous churches and monasteries by angry mobs.

Keen to assert his authority against the impertinent Protestants, Philip II sent an army to quell the revolt; however, the brutal way in which his men handled the situation even alienated some Dutch Catholics, and gradually the revolt became a fight for complete independence.

In 1579, seven northern regions formed the 'United Provinces of the Netherlands', asserting two years later that Philip II was no longer their rightful king, thus effectively declaring independence from Spain. Little did they imagine that their independence would only be fully recognised in

1648, after a devastating Europe–wide war. The southern provinces, including present-day Belgium and Luxembourg, remained loyal to Spain. Having been defeated by the Spanish and now in desperate straits, the United Provinces offered the Dutch crown to Elizabeth I of England and to the younger brother of the king of France. They both turned it down, although Elizabeth eventually sent a small army to help the rebels after William I of Orange was assassinated in 1584.

The English Reformation (1517–1558)

The Tudor king, Henry VIII, had ascended to the English throne in 1509, after the death of his elder brother, Arthur. Henry VIII married his brother's widow – Catherine of Aragon – but his roving eye soon fell upon another, and he tried to have his first marriage annulled, not understanding exactly how problematic this would become. Luther's ideas had already begun to spread to England, and received a warm reception from Henry VIII's new lover, Anne Boleyn. Henry VIII himself had initially vehemently defended the Church against the teachings of Luther, earning himself the title 'Defender of the Faith' in 1521.[65] This would soon change, however. Catherine had powerful allies: her nephew, Emperor Charles V, brought his influence to bear on the pope, who refused to annul the marriage. In turn, an embittered Henry refused to recognise papal authority.

As the Catholic faith did not recognise divorce, Henry VIII ordered the Archbishop of Canterbury to grant him one, which he duly did. This break with Rome was confirmed in 1534, when Henry was made Supreme Head of the English Church by an Act of Parliament. The head of the Church of England was henceforth to be the king, and those who challenged Henry VIII on this were executed. Those who supported him, on the other hand, were richly rewarded with lands and wealth confiscated from the Church after Henry

---

[65]   This title is still in use by English monarchs today.

VIII dissolved the monasteries. Royal revenues doubled in the process.

The king would eventually marry four more times, with the six marriages producing three heirs: Edward, Mary and Elizabeth. Each had differing religious beliefs. His son, Edward, was staunchly Protestant, but his reign was short. Mary, like her mother, Catherine of Aragon, was a devout Catholic, and when she became the first queen of England, she tried to re-establish Roman Catholicism. Whilst this was popular with some, any goodwill she had accrued was soon squandered. Her marriage to Philip II of Spain, the only son of Charles V, was particularly ill-advised. England, had no desire either to be ruled by a Spanish king, or to have its religious life run by the pope, and those who had benefited from the distribution of Church lands by Henry VIII certainly had no intention of returning them.

Mary's revival of heresy laws, and the public burnings that followed, were the final straw, earning her the epithet 'Bloody Mary'. To make matters worse, now allied with Spain, England was dragged into a war with France, losing Calais – the last territory it held in France – in 1558. When Mary died that same year, few mourned her loss. As Mary's marriage to Philip II had not produced an heir, the throne passed to her sister, Elizabeth, who would come to be regarded as one of England's greatest monarchs in a reign that lasted 45 years.

Elizabeth I: The Virgin Queen (1533–1603)

The new queen had Protestant sympathies for which she was eventually excommunicated by the pope, but she was not an extremist like her sister. Indeed, she was generally tolerant, except when her hand was forced. For example, when numerous plots were discovered, intending to put her Catholic first cousin, Mary, Queen of the Scots, on the English throne,

Elizabeth I felt she had no other choice but to have Mary executed.

With Elizabeth I's reign, England's status as a world power grew spectacularly. During this time, the first English attempts were made to set up a colony in northern America. Walter Raleigh named the land Virginia, after the virgin queen, at the suggestion of Elizabeth I herself, who may have hoped to curry favour with her Catholic subjects.

This claim on America, however, was the final straw for the Spanish, who, after all, had papal approval for their own claim on the entire continent. By sending aid to the United Provinces, by repeatedly attacking Spanish shipping and settlements and by executing her Catholic cousin, Elizabeth I had already given Spain ample provocation.

The Spanish immediately started preparations for sending an 'armada' of ships to invade England and restore the country to the Catholic faith. Word of this endeavour soon spread, as Philip II of Spain encouraged all Catholic countries to contribute funds and men. When it set sail, the Spanish Armada comprised 7,000 sailors, 17,000 soldiers and 130 ships. While the pope blessed the venture, the whole of Europe looked on. Yet despite the resources at its disposal, the Armada failed for a variety of reasons

First, there were delays when Francis Drake (known to the Spanish as 'Pirate Drake'!) sailed brazenly into the port of Cadiz in southern Spain, and sank 30 Spanish ships. This further infuriated Philip II.[66] Second, the man charged with leading the Armada – the Duke of Medina-Sidonia – had, rather unbelievably, never commanded a navy before, and sought desperately to relieve himself of the responsibility. Then,

---

[66] The event has gone into history as the 'Singeing of the King of Spain's Beard'.

a combination of factors – including Spanish mismanagement and unforced errors, poor weather, and being outmanoeuvred both by the ruthlessly opportunistic English tactics and their smaller, faster ships – ensured Spanish defeat. The Armada was forced to sail around the British Isles, battered by storms, and limped back to port in Spain with half of its ships and approximately half of its men lost – a financial disaster and a humiliating defeat.

While the inflow of wealth from the Americas helped Spain recover fairly rapidly from these financial losses, the country was less able to rebound from the blow to its prestige. To have suffered defeat at the hands of the upstart English and their Dutch allies was particularly galling for mighty Spain. Moreover, the defeat emboldened the English and Dutch to launch further maritime attacks on the Spanish, and contributed to their growth in power over the coming century. While the Armada's defeat, made Francis Drake a national hero, Elizabeth I herself became a legend: she had seen off the greatest threat the country had faced since the Norman invasion some 500 years earlier.

Although Elizabeth I added greatly to England's prestige, her successors unravelled much of what she had achieved. In 1603, James VI of Scotland – the son of Mary Queen of Scots – became James I of England, although it would take another century, and the Act of Union in 1707, before the two countries were officially joined to become the Kingdom of Great Britain.[67] James I was unloved by the people, and it was early in his reign, in 1605, that a group of Catholic peers, led by Guy Fawkes, plotted to blow up the Houses of Parliament – an

---

[67] This became the 'United Kingdom of Great Britain' only in 1801 with the addition of Northern Ireland.

act still remembered every year in England on 5th November. James I's son, Charles I, would lead the country to civil war.

The Thirty Years War and the Peace of Westphalia (1618-1648)

Philip II of Spain died in 1598, deeply in debt[68] and militarily exhausted. His successor, Philip III, had no choice but to call for a truce between Spain and the United Provinces of the Netherlands in 1609. The peace lasted nine years, only to be broken by a 30-year-long and Europe-wide religious war that lasted from 1618 to 1648, and involved most of the continental powers. Its alliances were not drawn solely along religious lines, however: despite having a Catholic king, the French Bourbons were conscious of their vulnerability, being surrounded by Habsburg territories, and fought alongside the Protestants.

Germany took the brunt of the attack, with entire regions devastated, and up to a quarter of the population killed by war, famine and disease. Other nations were bankrupted. Outside Europe, the war also raged in its fledgling colonies, with hostilities occurring in Asia, Africa and America. In the East, the Dutch waged a tough war against the Portuguese, ultimately depriving them of most of their possessions, including the lucrative Spice Islands.

Negotiations for peace began in 1643, but were only agreed upon five years later. The Peace of Westphalia, which was signed in 1648, marked both the end of the 80-year-long Dutch revolt and the Thirty Years War. Christianity, purportedly a religion of peace, had brought death and

---

68   Upon his death, the king owed up to 15 times the country's annual revenue.

destruction, and permanently divided Europe. It was clear to everyone that change was desperately needed.

The negotiations revealed a new Europe: the Dutch Republic was finally recognised as an independent state, and the territories of the Holy Roman Empire were accorded de facto sovereignty, thereby effectively reducing the power of the emperor. Such territorial adjustments, however, were in many ways merely incidental to the fundamental changes that occurred.

First, it was agreed that people should be allowed to express their religious opinions freely – a belief that continues to be the basis of civil society. Calvinism, Lutheranism and Catholicism were given equal recognition, and religion became separate from the state; it remains so in most Western countries to this day.[69] Second, the ratified edicts laid the foundations for modern-day sovereign nation states as opposed to imperial blocks, with kingship becoming the dominant form of government from that time on. It established boundaries for the states, many of which remain the same or similar today, and from this time onwards it would be national rivalry, rather than religious disputes, that would lead to wars and cause shifts in Europe's balance of power.

The Colonisation of North America

Over in North America, the European presence in the 16th century had been primarily focused on searching for a way to reach the Indies – still seen by many as the easiest path to

---

[69]   Pope Innocent X (1644-55) was appaled that Catholics had made peace with the heretical Protestants. Instead of welcoming peace, he declared the toleration of Protestantism and other articles of the Peace that displeased him 'null, void, invalid, iniquitous, unjust, damnable, reprobate, inane and altogether lacking force' and forbade Catholics to observe them.

wealth. America was not initially seen as a land to conquer and in which to settle, but more as a territory for settling the differences of the major European powers, and as a source of plunder with which to finance their wars.

By the mid-16th century Spain held most of central and southern America, benefiting from the huge amounts of silver it had mined there. Having enslaved and murdered a large proportion of the local population in their hunt for riches, the Spanish began to import slaves from Africa, hoping that they would prove both more resistant to disease and harder working. The Portuguese soon followed suit, importing slaves to man their sugar plantations in Brazil.

But as Spain grew rich, other powers sought ways to relieve her of her wealth, notably France, England and the Netherlands. England, under Elizabeth I, had specifically gained a reputation for piracy in the Caribbean, attacking the Spanish treasure galleons laden with gold and silver from the New World, thereby saving itself the effort and expense of mining them. With few riches discovered in northern America and the Caribbean, this area was of little interest to Spain, and so its enemies succeeded in gaining a foothold there.

Yet the European powers were slow to fully grasp the benefits of colonisation. It was not until 1565 that the Spanish founded a more substantial trading post on mainland America, at the city of St. Augustine in Florida. Twenty years later, Walter Raleigh also tried to establish such a permanent trading post on England's behalf at Roanoke Island, on the coast of present-day North Carolina. This was no easy endeavour though: the first colonists, feeling that the benefits of colonisation had been rather misrepresented to them, asked to be carried home the following year. The next would-be settlers to make the long journey across the Atlantic simply disappeared.

It was not until the early 17th century that a concerted effort was made by European powers to populate this part of the world. The effects of Religious persecution and bad harvests in early 17th century Europe provided plenty of volunteers.

Jamestown and the Settlement of North America (1607)

The failure at Roanoke, together with continued war with Spain, postponed English colonial efforts until 1606, when the king authorised the London Company to establish settlements. With the founding of Jamestown, Virginia, in 1607, came what many view as the true beginning of northern American colonial history. Even this was not easy, however; one third of the colonists died during the voyage, while another third perished in the first year in a period of adjustment that came to be called 'the seasoning'. Furthermore, the first 20 years were wracked by hunger and disease, requiring the settlers to be supplied by England until they could look after themselves. The colony was saved by growing tobacco, the smoking of which had become increasingly fashionable, and which was relatively easy to cultivate. It was not long before cheap Virginian tobacco flooded the markets.

The French founded their first permanent settlement in Quebec in 1608, and in 1609, Sir Henry Hudson, an English mariner in the pay of the Dutch, discovered Manhattan Island. The island was initially used as a base for traders, but the Dutch began to send settlers there in 1624, purchasing it from the native Americans (later known as Indians) for a few trinkets – a trade recognised as the best real estate deal in history. They named it New Amsterdam. Forty years later, the English decided New Amsterdam was blocking their westward expansion, so they captured it, and renamed it in honour of the Duke of York, brother of King Charles II. In return, and as part of the treaty to end the Anglo-Dutch war, the English ceded their South American territory in Suriname to the Dutch – possibly the worst real estate deal in history!

As word spread of the opportunities to be had in the Americas, more and more Europeans decided to emigrate. In 1610, on the other side of the continent, the Spanish founded the city of Santa Fe. In 1620, the Mayflower, carrying a group of religious separatists fleeing persecution in England, landed in Plymouth in present-day New England. A year later they celebrated the success of their first corn harvest, together with their Native American allies, in a thanksgiving ceremony still commemorated annually by Americans.

The Europeans soon earned a bad reputation among the Native Americans, whose names for them included 'people greedily grasping for land', or the 'coat-wearing people'. Over the course of the next few centuries, the indigenous population would be decimated by European diseases, principally smallpox and cholera.

The Europeans were generally surprised by the friendliness of the surviving natives, but butchered them nonetheless. Time and time again, the white settlers broke their treaties, while the Native Americans, not understanding why the newcomers needed any more land than was necessary for growing food, failed to unite against them. Eventually succumbing to both European diseases and their lust for land, they were slowly but surely dispossessed, subjugated and exterminated. There can be no question: this was genocide.

Things were not so different in South America, where those who had survived disease were often worked to death in mines or on farms by the Spanish and the Portuguese. It was the high death rate among the native populations that led Europeans to look for a new source of labour.

Sugar and the Slave Trade (15th–19th Centuries)

By the mid-15th century, slaves from Africa had been imported to Portugal in larger and larger numbers as a result of expeditions down the west African coast. There had been a centuries-long history of slave trading among native Africans and Arab middlemen prior to European intervention. Accustomed to the climate, and physically strong, African slaves had made good labourers in the sugar plantations of the recently established Portuguese colonies off the west African coast, including the Canaries, the Azores and Madeira.

It was this realisation that encouraged Portuguese entrepreneurs to begin exporting slaves to newly discovered Brazil, where they were put to work growing highly profitable sugarcane and mining silver. African slaves were imported in such huge numbers[70] that, by the end of the 17th century, up to half of Brazil's population consisted of African slaves.

Growing demand for sugar in Europe – a result of the increasing popularity of tea and coffee – encouraged other nations to grow sugarcane in the Caribbean, which had a similar climate to that of Brazil. This interest coincided with reduced returns on investment experienced by the tobacco-growing industry in the Caribbean after world markets were flooded by cheap Virginian tobacco. Moreover, mortality rates among the original European workforce in the Caribbean had been very high, and many of those who survived had fled to northern America, where the climate was more agreeable. Not only a new crop, but a new workforce would be needed.

While the English and the French busied themselves with setting up sugarcane plantations, the Dutch supplied the slaves and much of the financial backing in return for contracts to

---

[70]   Over three million Africans were exported to Brazil over the following 300 years.

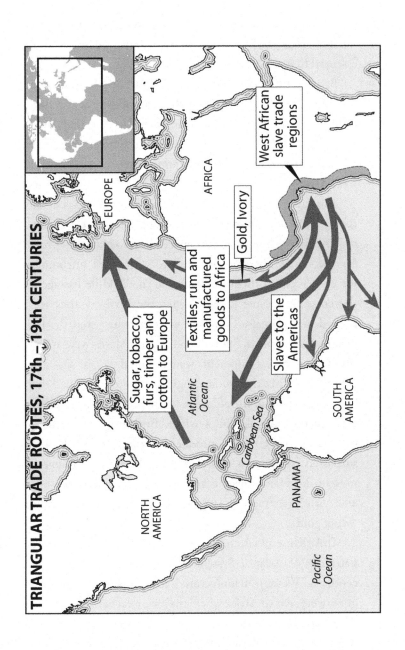

TRIANGULAR TRADE ROUTES, 17th – 19th CENTURIES

EUROPE

AFRICA

West African slave trade regions

Gold, Ivory

Textiles, rum and manufactured goods to Africa

Sugar, tobacco, furs, timber and cotton to Europe

Slaves to the Americas

Atlantic Ocean

Caribbean Sea

NORTH AMERICA

SOUTH AMERICA

PANAMA

Pacific Ocean

handle the sale of the sugar. Slaves were first supplied to northern America by the Dutch in 1619, eventually becoming essential to its economy.

By the time the 300-year-long slave trade ended, an estimated 50 percent of the roughly 15 million African slaves transported to the Americas as cheap labour had ended up in the Caribbean. In fact, up until the beginning of the 19th century, the majority of immigrants to the Americas were African.

The slaves' journey across the Atlantic from Africa generally took place under horrendous conditions. They were chained together in the hulls of overcrowded ships to maximise profits for the trader; disease was rife, and it was not uncommon for 25 percent of them to die during the 'Middle Passage', as the crossing became known. Once they arrived, they were treated like animals. Their low life expectancy and the lack of replacement in the population – most slaves were men – meant that regular shipments were required.

By the 1680s, the Dutch, English and French all had their own sugar plantation colonies, with production exceeding even that of Brazil. For a while, British-owned Barbados became the largest sugar producer in the world, only to be surpassed by Jamaica and French-held Santo Domingo in present-day Haiti. Entire islands became dependent on sugar, and with its extraordinary profitability, it came to be called 'white gold'.

This shameful commerce was part of the triangular trade pattern – or 'Atlantic System' – between the 17th and 19th centuries. Western manufactured goods, such as textiles and guns, were sent to Africa where they were exchanged for slaves who were, in turn, shipped to the Caribbean and exchanged for sugar and other commodities such as tobacco and coffee.

These were, in turn, sold in Europe, and used to buy manufactured goods that were subsequently exported to Africa, where the whole process repeated itself. A sugar by-product called molasses was distilled into rum, then shipped to Africa, creating a vicious cycle of profit whereby the fruits of slave labour were used to barter for more slaves.

Capital generated from sugar production and other slave-dependent industries was used to finance banks, extend credit and invest in new inventions, all of which contributed to the industrial revolution in Britain.

The Dutch Empire Grows...

Despite their seemingly never-ending war against Spain, the Dutch United Provinces developed a flourishing economy and a global empire. Building upon strong industries – grain-importing, fishing, and ship-building – and aided by the arrival of those fleeing religious persecution elsewhere in Europe, the Dutch were able not only to amass wealth, but also to devise ingenious solutions for managing it. The Bank of Amsterdam – the world's first central bank – was established in 1609, largely to finance trade. Good repayers of debt, the Dutch were able to get credit at advantageous interest rates, thereby allowing them to finance their wars and the expansion of their trade. Their investment in ship-building made them the world's most effective naval power until the late 17th century.

Pushed by Spanish embargoes to find new markets, the Dutch gained a strong presence in the Americas and in Asia, where the Dutch East India Company (established in 1602) became the first multinational corporation. Dutch privateers sacked Portuguese ships with impunity in both the Atlantic and Indian oceans, and succeeded in achieving a near monopoly on trade with the Spice Islands. Furthermore, in an attempt to protect their routes to the East, they established an outpost at the Cape of Good Hope, over which they would fight the English centuries later. The Dutch trading empire was the largest in the world – only later to be surpassed by England's – and would not be given up without a fight

...while Spain and Portugal Decline

The Portuguese and Spanish empires, on the other hand – united temporarily under Spanish rule from 1580 to 1640 – were on the wane. It was Portugal's misfortune to be united under the same crown as Spain at a time when Spain was waging war on half the world, and becoming increasingly isolated in the process. The side-effect of so many wars was bankruptcy, which Spain was forced to declare three times in the 16th century, in spite of its massive influx of wealth from the Americas. Yet Spain was also determined to stamp out any free thought or intellectual activity that might challenge Catholicism. With this aim, many books were banned,[71] students were forbidden to study abroad, and any foreign ideas were intrinsically unwelcome.

Fearful of change, the Iberian Peninsula[72] failed to develop at the same pace as the rest of Europe; by insulating itself against the Reformation, it missed out on the cultural and technological developments which had been so beneficial for its continental neighbours. Additionally, the flood of wealth from the New World – which, incidentally, led to unforeseen and serious inflation – actively discouraged innovation, as most goods could simply be bought.

---

[71]   The Jesuits, unfortunately, ran the printing presses.

[72]   Iberia is the part of Europe consisting of Spain and Portugal.

Portugal, under the House of Braganza, eventually reclaimed its independence from Spain in 1640, but by then it was too late for the country to regain its former glory. By this time, it had been weakened by the suppression of free thought, and had lost the pre-eminence in navigational techniques which had brought it such success.

France Gains Dominance Under Louis XIV

With Spain on the decline and England not yet in the ascendancy, France dominated European politics for much of the second half of the 17th century. Louis XIV was only five when he became king in 1643, but would be the longest-reigning monarch in European history (1643–1715). Louis XIV claimed rule by divine right, and famously proclaimed that he and the nation were one – *'L'état, c'est moi'*. His power was such that the 17th century even came to be known as the age of Louis XIV. To expand his empire, he married his first cousin, the daughter of King Philip IV of Spain. Yet despite its growing might, France was not without its own problems. Within France, Louis XIV – a strong Catholic – had to deal with considerable religious strife, and in 1685 revoked the Edict of Nantes, making Protestantism illegal. Beyond France's borders, the last decades of the 'Sun King' – a name derived from the emblem he chose to represent himself – were taken up with various wars which consumed much of the country's wealth.

England: The Beginnings of an Empire

During the 16th century England had only a fraction of the population and resources of either Spain or France. France was an historic foe, and the Netherlands were on their way to becoming England's main commercial enemy. England would make war and peace with both countries many times over the next hundred years. But England had advantages over other European countries, including the fact that, as an island, it was difficult to invade, and that its strong parliament had the ability to check the power of the king. Indeed, this latter factor would contribute to a devastating civil war between 1642 and 1651.

Like his father, Charles I was a strong believer in the divine right of kings, and for a time he refused to allow parliament to meet, recalling it only to raise money to fight the Scots, who had invaded England after Charles I's imposition of a new prayer book for their church services. His unsuccessful attempt, in 1642, to have five members of parliament arrested drove the country to civil war. This conflict was not between Catholics and Protestants, but rather between royalists – known as 'cavaliers' – and the opposition, who were known as 'roundheads', due to their short haircuts.

Oliver Cromwell, a puritanical member of parliament, became leader of the anti-royalist forces. He was instrumental in encouraging parliament to develop a professional army, which he would lead to victory on numerous occasions, both in England and Ireland. In 1649, having lost the Civil War, Charles I was executed, and four years later, Cromwell was appointed Lord Protector of the Commonwealth. Cromwell imposed military rule and led the country until he died in 1658. His son briefly replaced him, but Charles II, who had fled the country, spending his exile at the court of Louis XIV, was invited back in 1660 and reinstated as king of England, Scotland and Ireland. One of his first acts was to have Cromwell's body dug up and posthumously beheaded.

Charles II's reign was to see both the Great Plague in 1665, and the Great Fire of London in 1666, which destroyed some 13,000 homes. When Charles II died in 1685, he was succeeded by his brother, James II, who proceeded to appoint enough Catholics to senior positions in the realm to worry a predominantly Protestant parliament. As a result, parliament urged the Dutch prince, William of Orange – husband of James' daughter, Mary – to save England from a Catholic takeover.

When William landed in England in 1688 at the head of an army, James II – his father-in-law, and the last Catholic monarch to rule England – fled the country and sought sanctuary in France. After this bloodless revolution, William and Mary acceded as co-rulers in 1689, ruling the land together until Mary's death in 1694. From this time on, William ruled alone until his own death in 1702. James II's daughter, Anne, inherited the throne, but when she died in 1714, the Stuart royal line died with her. The crown passed to James I's great-grandson, the Elector of Hanover, who was invited to rule England as George I. He spoke German, but no English.

By copying the advanced banking system of the Netherlands, and by turning its attention west towards the Americas where the future lay, England gradually replaced the Netherlands as the world's economic and military superpower.

Japan Closes its Doors to the World (17th Century)

While Europeans were busy exploring the world, the Japanese had stopped travelling outside their country unless accompanying an army. In the 16th century, Japan had only just emerged from a lengthy period of anarchy and civil war, in which military governors – or Shoguns – managed the country in the name of the emperor. Under the last and most powerful Shogunate – founded by Tokugawa Ieyasu in 1603 and based in the city of Edo (present-day Tokyo) – Japan enjoyed some 250 years of peace.

The Portuguese had been the first Europeans to visit Japan in 1543. They were followed by other Europeans who were successful in introducing trade and Christianity to the islands, not to mention firearms. However, fearing military conquest by the Europeans and considering them a potential threat, the Japanese expelled them in the early 17th century. By 1635, Japanese citizens were forbidden from leaving the country, and those already abroad were not permitted back. In 1641, all trade with Europeans was limited to the port of Nagasaki, all foreign books were banned[73] and the country effectively locked out foreign interference for the next 200 years.

China expands under the Manchus

In neighbouring China, the Ming Dynasty eventually weakened under a series of mediocre emperors who were unable to deal with the growing threat of the rival Manchus from the north-east. Beijing – the home of the emperor – fell to a rebel army[74] in 1644, and Ming loyalists invited the Manchus to help recover the Imperial City. It was the Manchus who established the last Chinese imperial dynasty – the Qing (or Ching, meaning 'pure') – which would last for over 250 years, only coming to an end in 1911.

The Manchu population was a fraction of the size of the Chinese majority – with a different culture, language and writing – yet was successful in its domination. They insisted that all non-Manchu men shave their heads, leaving a long pigtail at the back as a sign of submission. They were also

---

[73] The ban was not revoked until 1720.

[74] The invasion of Beijing caused the last Ming emperor to hang himself.

incredibly successful in expanding the empire, managing to conquer Mongolia, and establishing a protectorate over what is now Tibet. It took them only 30 years to complete the conquest of China, including that of the island of Taiwan, the last outpost of anti-Manchu resistance.

Meanwhile in Russia...

Shortly after Japan effectively closed its doors to foreign interference, Russia made its first attempts at westernisation. In the mid-1600s Russia was vast, remote and underdeveloped. The country had little external trade and a weak military; several hundred years of Mongol rule had prevented the sort of social, intellectual and technological development that had characterised European countries during the same period. 'Russia had no or little exposure to the defining historical phenomena of Western civilisation: Roman Catholicism, feudalism, the Renaissance, the Reformation, overseas expansion, and colonisation.'[75] Despite this, the country had grown since the grand Duke of Moscow, Ivan III, had renounced his allegiance to the Mongol Khan in 1480 and assumed the title of Tsar. Since that time, Russian leaders had gradually moved eastwards, ruthlessly destroying any opposition.

Peter the Great, who ruled Russia between 1682 and 1725, is credited with a series of reforms that transformed Russia into a powerful modern state. A brush with the Ottoman Turks early in his reign encouraged Peter to seek support from various European powers that were also weary of Ottoman influence. As part of this endeavour, in 1697, Peter undertook

---

[75] *The Clash of Civilizations*, by Samuel Huntingdon.

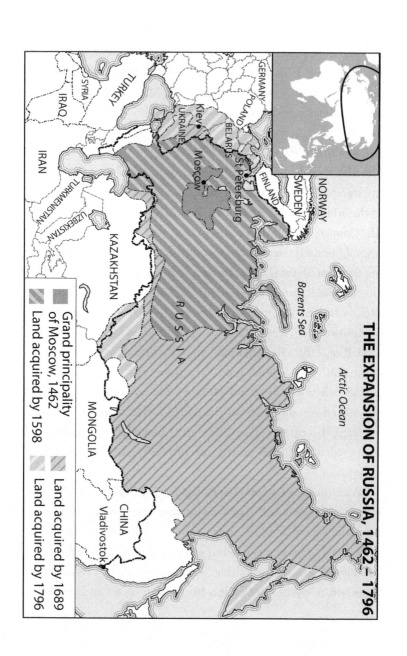

THE EXPANSION OF RUSSIA, 1462 – 1796

Grand principality
of Moscow, 1462
Land acquired by 1598

Land acquired by 1689
Land acquired by 1796

a 17-month tour of Europe, during which he visited many countries, including Germany, the Netherlands and England.

During his trip Peter learned how western European nations had used new technology and trade to gain power and wealth, and he was determined to do the same in Russia. On his return, he established a ship-building industry, modernised the army, reorganised the government, banned ancient dress, simplified the Russian alphabet, promoted education and even put a tax on beards – all in an attempt to westernise Russian and drag it out of the Middle Ages. Yet Peter also had many faults: he might well have been a progressive visionary, but he was also a ruthless leader who had his own son tortured and murdered, and caused the deaths of thousands of workers in his determination to build the city of St Petersburg on marshland.

One of Peter's main goals was to gain access to the Baltic Sea and its trade through establishing a warm-water port, which Russia lacked. In 1700, after making a secret alliance with Denmark and Poland, he marched into the Baltic region, thereby inciting war with Sweden. Its young king, Charles XII, initially won a series of battles, which gave him a reputation as a great military man, but eventually lost the 21-year-long 'Great Northern War'. Russia gained new territory, and Tsar Peter was declared 'Peter the Great and Emperor of all Russia'. Under his orders, the capital was moved from Moscow to Saint Petersburg. Sweden lost its supremacy as the leading power in the Baltic region, and Russia's growth 'alerted other powers to the fact that the hitherto distant and somewhat barbarous Muscovite state was intent upon playing a role in European affairs.'[76]

After Peter's death in 1725, Russia was ruled for all but a few of the next 70 years by women, including Catherine the

---

[76]   *The Rise and Fall of the Great Powers* by Paul Kennedy, Fontana Press.

Great – the German wife of Peter's grandson. During this time, Russia continued to expand, extending its borders well into central Europe, but failing to keep up with the rapidly developing West. Following Peter's lead, Catherine flirted with reform, but changed her mind when Louis XVI of France was executed during the French Revolution. However, this lack of reform in Russia would lead to ever-increasing discontent and, with time, to revolution.

The Kingdom of Prussia (1701–1871)

West of Russia, the 1648 Peace of Westphalia had divided the Holy Roman Empire into 300 different principalities. One of these, Prussia, became its own kingdom in 1701, growing in power under its first king, Frederick I. When his son, Frederick II (Frederick the Great), inherited the crown in 1740, he also inherited the most advanced army in Europe. Wishing his Hohenzollern Dynasty to become as great as that of the French Bourbons and the Austrian Habsburgs, whose rivalry dominated European politics in the 18th century, he took the opportunity to put his army to the test in two major conflicts. One arose over the succession of the Austrian Habsburg emperor, Charles VI, and became an expensive stalemate. He initiated another in 1756, after occupying land that lay between Austria and his own borders.

These wars made Prussia and Russia into the new superpowers, overtaking Spain and the Netherlands. Poland had the misfortune of being sandwiched between the two, and was eventually partitioned between them, ceasing to exist as an independent country, and only regaining its autonomy after the First World War.

Frederick II could not have anticipated, however, that his land grab would initiate a major conflict that would involve all the leading European powers. It would even eventually spill over into America, where the huge costs and consequences of the Anglo-French war would ultimately lead to the American War of Independence and to the French Revolution.

The Seven Years War (1756–1763)

Since 1754 there had been considerable animosity between the French and the British over the possession of territories in America, and over control of the lucrative fur trade. With the eruption of conflict in Europe, open war also finally broke out in America in 1756. With substantial support from the Native Americans, whom the British had badly alienated, the French initially seized the advantage. In 1758 the tide turned, however, under William Pitt – the Secretary of State and future Prime Minister – who had been assigned responsibility for war. A great orator and confident of his own abilities, Pitt stated, 'I know that I can save this country, and that no one else can.'

Through its unparalleled maritime expertise, the British navy destroyed the French fleet in 1759, thereby hampering France's ability to supply its troops in America. When Montreal and Quebec fell to the British, the writing was on the wall. By 1760 the whole of French Canada was in British hands and the war was effectively won, although a peace treaty to end it was not signed until 1763. Concerned about the balance of power, the Spanish had finally supported the French in 1762, but their assistance came too late, and they lost Cuba to the British for their pains.

The consequences of the war in America were enormous: Britain gained all of northern America east of the Mississippi, which included taking Canada from the French and Florida

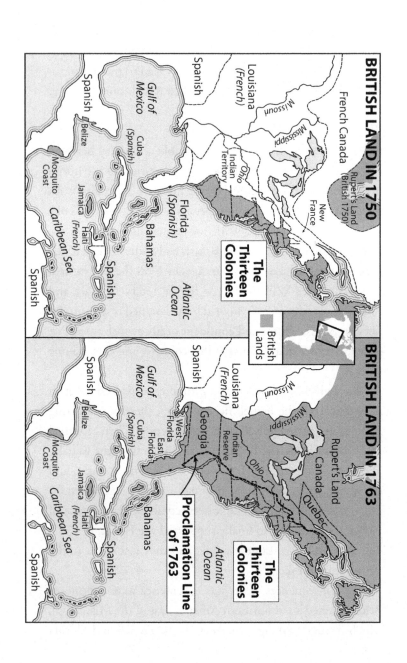

from the Spanish[77]. With its empire thus vastly increased, it emerged as the greatest colonial power. France, on the other hand, was defeated on every front, having to relinquish all its territory in mainland America with the exception of New Orleans, and retaining only a few sugar islands in the Caribbean. This saw not only the end of France's American empire, but also the end of its political and cultural influence in the region.

Any joy felt by the 13 British colonies at having rid themselves of the French threat was dampened by a royal proclamation in 1763, forbidding their colonising of American Indian lands to the west of the Appalachian Mountains. The increasing dissatisfaction with British rule felt by frontiersmen, land speculators and colonists in general – and the inability of the British to quell it – became a tinderbox. Another decade would pass, however, before the fatal spark ignited it.

The Europeans Dominate India

The effects of Seven Years War had also been felt in India, where the British expelled the French. The Mughals – a Persian rendering of the word Mongols – had ruled much of India since 1526, when the Muslim prince, Babur – who descended from both Tamerlane and Genghis Khan – conquered northern India, defeating the Delhi Sultan at the Battle of Panipat. The Mughal Empire had reached its height under Babur's grandson Akbar, who, through his enlightened views and religious tolerance, became known as Akbar the Great.

The English had taken advantage of the stability of Akbar's rule by means of the East India Company (EIC), a trading company founded in 1600 under Elizabeth I which

---

[77] The Spanish exchanged Florida for Cuba.

had been assigned a monopoly on all trade with Asia. The EIC rapidly focussed on India after it became apparent that Dutch pre-eminence in trade with the Spice Islands would thwart any attempts to gain a foothold there. Why wage a spice war that they would probably lose when plenty of trade was to be had in India? This happened to coincide with a huge increase in European demand for Indian cotton cloth, which was inexpensive, washable and lightweight compared to the itchy wool that was ubiquitous in Europe at the time. Before long, the EIC had established trading posts along the Indian coast, with the main ones – Bombay, Madras and Calcutta – eventually developing into major cities.

When the Mughal overlords imposed a less tolerant form of Islam, they alienated many of the indigenous Hindu majority. A number of regional states rebelled and sought support from the British and the French, richly rewarding both for providing aid. It was the rivalry between the French and the English that allowed the EIC to extend its control over more and more of India.

The French and the British fought each other several times in the 1740s and 1750s, until Robert Clive – who became known as Clive of India – led the British to a decisive victory over the French at the Battle of Plassey[78] in 1757. This French defeat crucially allowed the EIC to gain dominance in India, with the substantial compensation they levied from the Bengali treasury financing further British expansion and eventually enabling them to put their own candidate on the Mughal throne. For the next hundred years, the EIC invested in the infrastructure of India, hoping that such expenditure would facilitate trade.

---

[78] Plassey is an anglicised version of 'Palashi', which is located about 150km north of Calcutta.

The Hindu Religion

Hinduism is the world's oldest existing religion. Although its origins are unclear, it is believed to have originated in or near the Indus Valley in northern India some 4,000 years ago, and the vast majority of its followers are still found in India to this day.[79] Unlike other major religions, Hinduism has no founder or prophets. Its adherents believe in a supreme God, called Brahman, who takes on many qualities and forms, represented by a number of deities which all emanate from him.

Hindus believe in reincarnation: an endless cycle of birth, death and rebirth, driven by how one has lived one's previous life. According to Hindu belief, at some point mankind will learn from its mistakes and bring an end to suffering. This, in turn, will bring final salvation. For thousands of years, Hinduism enforced a hierarchical and discriminatory caste system driven by superstition, tradition and religious beliefs, and this still lingers on today. It has even been suggested that the sense of fatalism engendered by the caste system throttled initiative, and that this may have played a part in the ease with which both the Mughals and the British managed to dominate India.

The American War of Independence (1775-1783)

Despite the money flowing in from India, Britain nevertheless struggled to meet the huge cost of the Seven Years War, and the defence of its colonies in America became a burden. The British government sought various ways making the colonies contribute to their own defence, from taxing sugar to requiring all legal documents to be stamped for a price. However, it was forced to repeal several of these acts, as the American colonies rejected taxes levied by a government in which they had no representation.

---

[79] Up to 80 percent of Indians currently confess themselves to be Hindu.

Ironically, it was the repeal of a tax, not its imposition, that caused the greatest conflagration. The EIC owed the British government taxes, but were having to compete with smugglers importing tea into America illegally, thereby depressing legal sales, which delayed the repayment of these arrears. The ability to export tea directly to America – thereby avoiding paying tax on it in London – would allow the EIC to lower its price and boost sales, which would, in turn, speed up the repayment of its back taxes. However, whilst the EIC no longer had to pay tax on tea in London, the American colonists were taxed on any EIC tea they bought. With the revenue going to the British government, this was seen to constitute 'taxation without representation'.

A group of opponents to British rule and smugglers, who were concerned with their business prospects, dumped 340 chests of EIC tea into Boston Harbour in December 1773 as a sign of protest. The 'Boston Tea Party', as it became known, was met with a vigorous response from London: the harbour was closed, and British troops were dispatched to impose order and enforce obedience to parliament – a highly significant act for a population used to relying on the army for its defence.

In April 1775, the British army went to seize a cache of arms in Concorde – a small, north-eastern coastal town near Boston. Shots were fired, and the American Revolution began. American colonists declared their independence on 4th July 1776, but it would take eight years of brutal battle before Britain would finally recognise that it had lost.

The war's duration was the result of neither side's willingness to submit. In the end, it was a combination of a 3,000-mile-long supply line, terrible winters to which they were unaccustomed and sheer bad luck which defeated the British. The Americans had been fortunate to have the brilliant leadership of George Washington, who went on to become the first president of the United States of America in 1789. To make matters worse, the French, the Spanish and the Dutch all declared war on Britain. Little did the British know that they would not see peace until 1815; little did the French know that aiding a people at war with its rulers would come back to bite them.

In the 1783 peace settlement that officially ended the war, the Americans received all the land between Canada and Florida east of the Mississippi. It is worth noting that while American territory doubled (and would double again when they bought Louisiana from the French in 1803), at that point, Spain still ruled more territory in the Americas than the Americans themselves.

Terra Australis Incognita

One unintended consequence of the American Revolution was a focus on populating Australia. From the time of antiquity, people had thought that *Terra Australis Incognita* – or 'unknown land of the south' – existed as a counterweight to the continents north of the equator. Already occupied by Aborigines for some 50,000 years, Australia had been cut off from the rest of the world by rising sea levels following the last ice age. It was not until 1606 that Europeans first became aware of the continent after a Dutchman, Willem Janszoon, landed on the west coast while seeking new trade routes to the East. However, he failed to realise that it was a separate continent.

In 1644 another Dutchman, Abel Tasman, explored the northern part of the continent and named it New Holland – a name it would bear for over a hundred years.

Tasman had also previously discovered New Zealand in 1642 – originally named *Nieuw Zeelandia*, most probably after the Dutch province of Zeeland – but Tasman never set foot on the island, and the Dutch never followed up on this discovery.

Australia wasn't colonised by the Dutch for two main reasons. First, they were more interested in trade with the established Asian markets. Moreover, the land seemed very dry and barren, so was predominantly used as a navigational aid in the journey from Europe to the East Indies, or otherwise as a stopping point for taking on fresh water. Second, the 17th century was so fraught with war between the European powers that the Dutch simply lacked the resources with which to colonise a new continent.

It was not until 1770 that Captain James Cook, having already claimed New Zealand for the British Crown in 1769, did the same for Australia, landing on the hitherto unexplored east coast, and naming the territory New South Wales. When it became clear that the American colonies – which had previously served as a dumping ground for prisoners – were winning their War of Independence, Australia began to be promoted as somewhere for Britain to rid itself of its unwanted criminals.

In January 1788, a penal colony was set up near Port Jackson (later to be renamed Sydney, after the British Home Secretary) to house the 736 convicts who had left England eight months previously. With the prisoners came a number of entrepreneurs seeking adventure and hoping to take advantage of an inexpensive labour force. Thus began the proper settlement of Australia.

The indigenous Aborigines were treated in the same way as other peoples who had been encountered by European settlers elsewhere in the world – with murderous contempt. It was not uncommon for them to be hunted like animals, and their numbers were further diminished by European diseases to which they had no immunity.

It was not until 1840 that the Maori – the indigenous people of New Zealand – accepted British sovereignty under the Treaty of Waitangi and became British subjects. Both Australia and New Zealand developed into major sources of wool and wheat for Britain and would later provide troops to support it during the world wars of the 20th century. Both countries remain tied to Britain to this day as part of the British Commonwealth.

VI

THE MODERN PERIOD

The French Revolution (1789–1799)

The war that had helped the American colonies become independent from Britain also cost the French crown dearly. In purely financial terms, the French king, Louis XVI, was forced to look for new ways to fund state expenditure. Specifically, the king was keen to end the tax exemptions that the Church (the First Estate) and the nobility (the Second Estate) had hitherto enjoyed. Unsurprisingly, they resisted this. Louis then convened the nearest thing France had to a parliament, the Estates-General, which included the Third Estate (peasants, middle class and urban workers), who made up over 95 percent of the population. When the Estates-General finally met in May 1789 – not having done so since 1614 – there were great hopes for reform: at the time, the greatest tax burden was borne by the growing middle classes, who hoped the parliament would give them a greater voice.

However, things did not go according to plan for the king. When it became apparent that the nobility and clergy held an unfair monopoly on voting rights, those who represented the Third Estate broke away to form their own National Assembly, taking up the slogan '*Liberté, Egalité, Fraternité*' and vowing not to disperse until France had a constitution that gave them the recognition they felt they deserved. At the same time, a series of bad harvests had caused the price of bread – the staple diet of many – to rise. Fuelled by the writings of French enlightenment philosophers, who throughout the 18th century had challenged the old assumptions about society, religion and justice, revolutionary zeal took hold of the people.

At one point, alarmed by rumours of an army gathering near the king's residence at Versailles, outside Paris, the mob was urged to arm itself for its own defence. In an effort to gain supplies of guns and gunpowder, the mob stormed the Bastille – the main prison in Paris – on 14th July. While the prison held only seven inmates at the time, the event represented a symbolic attack on the king's authority, and the date is generally accepted as the beginning of the French Revolution.

The king vacillated, but eventually gave in to the people's demands to replace his army with their own militia. When he and his Austrian wife, Marie Antoinette, were moved – supposedly 'under protection' by the National Guard – from Versailles to central Paris, they realised that it was in their interests to flee. They eventually did so in June 1791. However, despite disguising themselves, they were recognised a mere 20km from the border and returned to Paris, where they were duly imprisoned. The newly formed French Republic eventually executed the king in January 1793, and the queen suffered the same fate nine months later. From that point onwards, 'the revolution in France had become war in Europe: not an old-fashioned, familiar kind of war between monarchs for territory, but a newer ideological war between peoples and kings for the ending of old institutions and the fulfilment of dreams of a new society'.[80]

The shock was felt throughout Europe: a king had been murdered by his own people. What's more, the revolution threatened to spread beyond the borders of France. When Austria – ruled by Marie Antoinette's brother, the Holy Roman

---

[80]   *Europe since Napoleon* by David Thomson, Penguin.

Emperor, Leopold II – refused to extradite French émigrés accused of plotting against the revolution, France declared war. Nations across Europe, fearful of how the revolution's message might damage their own authority, joined forces in an alliance against France, beginning a war that would spread across the globe and cause terrible suffering for more than 20 years.

With the country surrounded by enemies, extremists rapidly gained power in France; anyone who spoke against the revolution was declared an enemy of the people and sent to the guillotine. Ironically, Maximilien Robespierre and Georges Danton, two of the leaders responsible for initiating this so-called 'Reign of Terror', also became its victims in 1794.

Napoleon Bonaparte: Emperor of the French (1799–1815)

Filled with revolutionary fervour, the French rapidly won a number of stunning victories. The exploits of one young Corsican officer, Napoleon Bonaparte, gained such public recognition that in 1799, at the age of 30, he was able to seize power and establish a military dictatorship with little opposition; even when his attempt to conquer Egypt and block Britain's route to India failed at the Battle of the Nile, the French fleet was ingloriously defeated by the British under Admiral Horatio Nelson – it was not held against him. Five years later, Napoleon became emperor of the French. He invited the pope to crown him in the cathedral of Notre Dame in Paris, but famously placed the crown on his own head at the last minute as a sign that he was in control not only of France, but also of his own destiny.

The British continued to frustrate Napoleon's ambitions, however. Most notably, at the Battle of Trafalgar – off the coast of south-west Spain – in 1805, they destroyed or captured two thirds of the combined French and Spanish fleet without losing a single vessel, although Admiral Nelson, who again led the British fleet was mortally wounded. Despite this defeat at sea, the French continued to have great success on land, defeating Austrian, Russian and Prussian armies in quick succession.

Increasingly concerned by the possibility of Europe becoming unified under a hostile power, the British organised a new anti-French coalition – an act which naturally infuriated Napoleon. Unable to invade Britain while the British navy commanded the English Channel, Napoleon sought to implement a blockade of British goods, forbidding their import into any part of Europe either under his control or in alliance with him, and declaring open season on all British ships. He hoped that this action would force Britain to sue for peace.

Most countries fell into line, but the Portuguese – long-standing allies of Britain – proved intransigent. This provided Napoleon with a reason to invade the Iberian Peninsula in 1808, and place his brother, Joseph, on the Spanish throne. The king of Portugal fled to his colony in Brazil, which he established as the temporary capital of the Portuguese Empire. To Napoleon's dismay, the Spanish did not accept a French king and, aided by the British, the entire Iberian Peninsula became a persistent problem for him, successfully distracting his attention when it needed to be focused elsewhere.

Despite these setbacks, however, by 1812 Napoleon controlled a quarter of Europe's population, and members of his family occupied thrones in Spain, Naples and Holland, creating a new dynastic family in Europe. He even took as his wife Marie Louise – the Habsburg daughter of the Austrian emperor Francis I, and niece of Marie Antoinette, the murdered queen of France.

Yet it was not only the Portuguese who refused to cooperate; the Russians also continued to trade with Britain. Suspecting Russia's imperial intentions, Napoleon invaded the country in the summer of 1812 with approximately half a million men, but the Russians adopted a scorched-earth policy, depriving Napoleon of the ability to feed his army. The effects of disease and desertion were exacerbated by an inconclusive battle at Borodino, just outside Moscow, in which some 50,000 of his soldiers were killed. When Napoleon succeeded in reaching Moscow, only 100,000 of his men remained.

Worse still, when it finally became clear to Napoleon that the Russians had no intention of surrendering, his army was forced into a retreat during the Russian winter. Where desertion and hunger had failed, 'General Winter' and 'General Typhus' succeeded. Of the half a million men who had set out, only some 20,000–40,000 returned. Huge numbers of horses were also lost – some estimate as many as 200,000 – contributing directly to Napoleon's defeats over the coming years, in a world in which a strong cavalry could make or break a battle.

Like that of the Habsburgs before it, Napoleon's growing empire was a threat to other European powers. Encouraged by his defeat in Russia, these powers formed yet another alliance against him, advancing together on Paris where, in 1814, Napoleon was forced to surrender. He was sent to exile on the Mediterranean island of Elba, which was effectively accorded to him as a sovereign principality, along with an income and the retention of his title. Not one to give up easily though, Napoleon escaped from the island, managed to assemble a huge army of loyal soldiers while marching north through France and waged a final war in Europe.

But his time had passed. He was finally and decisively beaten in 1815 by an allied army, led by the Duke of Wellington at the Battle of Waterloo[81] near Brussels in present-day Belgium. This time he was banished to the island of St. Helena in the south Atlantic, under British guard and far enough away for him never to cause trouble again. He lived peacefully for another six years before dying of cancer in 1821, at the age of 51.

Napoleon's thirst for power had led to death and destruction, and, 'far from establishing a united Europe under French command, he accelerated the growth of nationalism which would eventually lead to the First 'World War'.[82] Nevertheless, his numerous reforms changed the way in which Europe was run: he introduced a legal code that serves as the basis for the legal system in many European countries today, and his regime challenged the institutions and beliefs of the old order. For better or for worse, he brought the secularism of the revolution into mainstream thought. It is to Napoleon's campaigns in Egypt that we owe the discovery of the Rosetta Stone, which allowed us to translate ancient Egyptian hieroglyphics – a discovery that subsequently opened up the world of Egyptian history to mankind.

The Industrial Revolution

Britain was not without its own revolution in the 18th century, albeit one of a different kind. A major turning point in human history, some have gone so far as to call the Industrial Revolution the most far-reaching and influential

---

[81]   Despite the Duke of Wellington calling it a 'damned close run thing'.

[82]   *A Concise History of the Modern World* by William Woodruff, 2010, reproduced with permission of Palgrave MacMillan.

transformation of human society since the advent of agriculture.

Early 18th-century Britain, and most of the world for that matter, was predominantly agricultural, with economic activity focused on the products of farming – chiefly crops and wool. Britain had a small population of five million, and a modest life expectancy. Malnutrition and famine were common. Moreover, the only sources of power were wind, water, horsepower and manual labour. A person in 1750 could travel no faster than Caesar had 1,800 years previously.

In many ways, however, Britain was in a good position compared with its continental neighbours. Geographically, 'the steady shift in the main trade routes from the Mediterranean to the Atlantic and the great profits that could be made from colonial and commercial ventures in the West Indies, North America, the Indian subcontinent, and the Far East naturally benefited a country situated off the western flank of the European continent'.[83] For a long time, Britain had a monopoly on trade with its northern American colonies which, as with Britain's other colonies, provided both a supply of raw materials and demand for manufactured goods. The economy had become global, and London had taken its place at its centre.

Closer to home, Britain also benefited from large deposits of easily accessible coal and iron ore, the two natural resources upon which industrialisation would come to depend; the laissez-faire attitude of its government, which encouraged innovation and trade; and a risk-taking private sector with capital to invest. Finally, an absence of internal duties on

---

[83]   *The Rise and Fall of the Great Powers* by Paul Kennedy, Fontana Press.

commerce meant that, compared to mainland Europe, moving goods internally was relatively inexpensive.

Britain was also on the verge of an unprecedented population explosion. Agricultural reform had encouraged larger farms, thereby increasing agricultural output, which led to cheaper food. People's diets also improved thanks to regular imports of meat from the colonies. Advances in medical knowledge and sanitation meant that fewer people died in infancy, and the average lifespan also increased. Importantly, lower food prices meant that people did not have to spend everything they earned on eating, and could therefore purchase other products. This subsequently led to increasing pressure to produce a greater volume of manufactured goods, of which the most sought-after were textiles.

Demand for cotton – both from within Britain and from its colonies – was virtually unlimited, as cotton was much smoother and kinder to the skin than wool; it was also longer lasting, cheaper and much easier to clean. The scale of cotton imports was such that England banned the importing of cotton cloth from India in 1700 in an attempt to prop up its own wool industry. Businesses responded by importing raw cotton which could be spun, then woven in Britain. This increased the competition for labour, which became more expensive, thereby raising production costs.

It was this combination of increasing labour costs and surging demand that led merchants to explore ways of reducing their costs, rather than increasing their prices, in order to become more competitive. Machines were developed to speed up production, helping to make local cotton not only cheaper, but also finer and stronger than Indian cotton. However, the industry became a victim of its own success: demand increased to such an extent that the supply of raw cotton could not keep up. The problem was only solved when an American, Eli Whitney, invented the cotton gin.[84] This machine enabled a worker to clean 50 times more cotton than normal.

Despite these great improvements, it was the application of the steam engine to the textile industry that really drove the revolution and changed the face of society. Initially developed in the early 1700s to pump water from coal mines, the steam engine was improved upon in the 1760s by James Watt, a Scottish engineer whose name was later borrowed to define a unit of power: the watt. Two decades later, Watt developed a rotary engine that could power machines to spin and weave cotton cloth. The new methods, which increased the quantity of goods produced while decreasing the costs, sounded the death knell for handlooms.[85]

In coal, British industry had found a cheap and efficient source of power to take over from dwindling supplies of wood and its by-product, charcoal. Iron makers began to prefer using coal rather than wood charcoal, as it burned hotter and more cleanly. As more and more machines were manufactured from iron – which was also used to build railway lines, trains and ships – the demand for coal increased. The revolution might well have failed, or at the very least been significantly slower, had Britain not been blessed with an abundant supply of coal.

With the scope for making increasingly large profits expanding at an unprecedented rate, industrial capitalists became a force to be reckoned with. In order to maximise their returns, many of them invested their capital into the

---

[84]   The word 'gin' in this instance comes from the word 'engine'.

[85]   Not everyone was happy that skilled workers were being replaced by unskilled ones, who were simply required to manage machinery. A group that came to be called Luddites resisted the introduction of new machines by smashing them. The term Luddite is now equated with anyone who resists new technology.

infrastructure required to improve the transport of both coal and finished products. Canals, railways and roads all received significant investment. Steam-powered vessels that did not rely on wind for their propulsion gradually replaced less reliable sailing ships, and steam-powered locomotives revolutionised transport on land.

The improved transportation network, and the economies of scale that resulted from mass-production, put more products within the reach of more people at prices they could afford. The result was a huge boost to the economy. It is even argued that the resulting increase in tax revenue played a large part in the ability of Britain to defeat Napoleon, as it provided funds on a scale which the French could not match.

There were also profound changes in social structure, with an unprecedented movement of people from the countryside to towns. Initially this was caused by displaced peasants – whose manual labour had been superseded by new agricultural techniques – migrating to towns reactively in search of better-paid work. However, the growing demand for manufactured goods required a labour force of its own, and people soon began relocating to towns in their millions. Enormous cities developed around manufacturing centres, and by 1850 most Englishmen were working in industrial towns. These towns, however, were unprepared for such a large population influx, and this brought its own distinct new set of problems.

Rule Britannia: Great Britain Leads the World (1815–1900)

Britain profited greatly from France's defeat in 1815, gaining various territories including the Cape of Good Hope and the strategic islands of Malta, Mauritius and Ceylon (Sri Lanka). The blockade on trading with Britain imposed by Napoleon on his European allies ironically served to give Britain a monopoly on overseas trade, allowing it to expand even further. Additionally, Britain's newly acquired territories increased the number of markets for British goods whilst simultaneously providing raw materials to feed its growth. By 1850, Britain dominated world trade in manufactured goods, supplying two thirds of the globe with cotton from the industrial centres of northern England. It was also predominant in related services such as shipping, finance and insurance, with the result that London became the largest city in the world. By the turn of the century, the British Empire had acquired territories on five continents: Queen Victoria ruled about 20 percent of the world's landmass.

From about 1830, the Industrial Revolution gradually spread from Britain, through Europe and to the United States. Other countries were slower to industrialise, however. France could no longer compete: any nascent industrial development had been interrupted by the French Revolution in 1789, and this hiatus only ended with Napoleon's defeat in 1815, at which point the country was stripped of much of its empire. Even after 1815, the country remained firmly focused on agriculture and had limited coal supplies, a poor transportation structure and immature financial markets.

Germany enjoyed an abundance of coal, but was still not unified, consisting of a patchwork of 38 separate states of the former Holy Roman Empire, of which Austria and Prussia were the largest. Their failure to co-operate with each other did not lend itself to national progress.

From a position of maritime supremacy and technological leadership in the 17th century, the Netherlands had begun a period of slow decline from the 18th century onwards, partly due to having sunk all their capital into spices and slaves as opposed to the growing textile industry. The Netherlands lost its colonies in the Americas, and the costs of running its colonies in Asia eventually outweighed the value of what they produced. The Dutch had also suffered from being dragged into several wars – due to both trading conflicts and disputed royal successions – during the 18th century. In 1795, French troops commanded by Napoleon overran the country, forcing the Dutch to pay significant sums for garrisoning them. Finally, seemingly fixated on commerce, Dutch investors preferred to lend to financial markets rather than to invest in industry, just when investment in industry would become the distinguishing mark of a strong state.

Russia, for its part, still lacked a middle class, which was vital for successful industrialisation, and despite the advantage of having a huge population, 'remained technologically backward and economically underdeveloped. Extremes of climate and the enormous distances and poor communications partly accounted for this, but so also did severe social defects: the military absolutism of the tsars, the monopoly of education in the hands of the Orthodox Church, the venality and unpredictability of the bureaucracy, and the institution of serfdom, which made agriculture feudal and static'.[86]

In North America, farming and trading took precedence over industrial production until the 1820s and 1830s, and even then, industrialisation was essentially confined to the north. For a long time, the richest people in the US were southern cotton farmers who had no incentive to reinvest their profits into machinery when they could exploit slave labour. Asia had the same issue: labour was so cheap that there was little incentive to invest in machines.

---

[86]   *The Rise and Fall of the Great Powers* by Paul Kennedy, Fontana Press.

The turning point for mainland Europe's efforts to catch up with industrialised Britain was an increase in population, which resulted in both a larger market and a growing labour supply.

The Growth of Socialism

But industrialisation also had a darker side. The European urban infrastructure had been unprepared for the rise in numbers that followed the rapid growth in industry. The side effects of this were serious overcrowding, disease, poverty and unrest – a state of affairs highlighted by the popular press. Socialist ideology arose from the desire to redress the inequity of situation between those who toiled in the new factories of Europe and those who owned them, taking all the profits.

Settling in England after having been expelled from numerous countries in Europe, Karl Marx wrote two works that subsequently formed the basis of socialist thought: *The Communist Manifesto* and *Das Kapital*. He stated that the history of society could be considered as a history of class struggles, as opposed to conflict between states or individuals. He theorised that the workers would finally revolt against the business owners – or bourgeoisie – thereby ending the era of class struggles: 'The proletarians have nothing to lose but their chains. They have a world to win. Working men of all countries, unite!' Industrial capitalism would collapse and be replaced by a communist society, in which different social classes would not exist. Largely unread until the 1870s, his work became the main inspiration for communist regimes in the 20th century.

The Independence of South America (1808–1826)

The American and French revolutions of the 18th century, and the subsequent Napoleonic wars in Europe that continued into the 19th century, also had monumental consequences for South America. In 1800, South America remained almost entirely in Spanish and Portuguese hands, yet within 26 years, all that remained of these European empires in the New World were the Spanish-held Caribbean islands of Cuba and Puerto Rico. Even these would become protectorates of the USA after the Spanish-American war of 1898.

Spain's restrictions over economic matters, the authoritarian nature of its government, and the preferential status accorded to those born in Spain over Creoles (those with Spanish parentage but born in the Americas) caused significant local resentment and gave rise to revolutionary factions. Napoleon's invasion of the Iberian Peninsula in 1808 gave such movements the excuse and the impetus they needed to throw off the yoke of their colonial masters. Led by freedom fighters such as Simon Bolivar[87] – the George Washington of Latin America, after whom the country of Bolivia was named – and Jose de San Martin, who led the liberation of Argentina and Chile, most of Spanish-held South America had gained its independence by 1825.

The local population of Brazil °only sought their independence after Napoleon was finally defeated in 1815, when the Portuguese royal family returned to Lisbon after their seven-year exile. In a relatively bloodless coup, Brazil gained its independence in 1822 – with the son of the Portuguese monarch as emperor – but would become a republic only in 1889.

The freedom these people gained was not entirely that which they had hoped for: with little experience of managing

---

[87]   Bolivar also became known as El-Libertador, Spanish for 'the Liberator'.

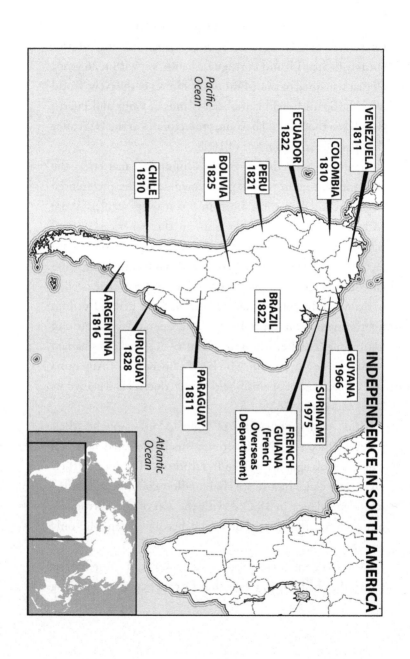

INDEPENDENCE IN SOUTH AMERICA

Pacific Ocean

Atlantic Ocean

VENEZUELA 1811

ECUADOR 1822

COLOMBIA 1810

BOLIVIA 1825

PERU 1821

CHILE 1810

BRAZIL 1822

ARGENTINA 1816

URUGUAY 1828

PARAGUAY 1811

GUYANA 1966

SURINAME 1975

FRENCH GUIANA (French Overseas Department)

their own affairs, the majority of the countries rapidly became military dictatorships.

The Rise of Nationalism and Liberalism

At the Congress of Vienna in 1815, it seemed initially that the old order would be restored. Exhausted after 25 years of warfare, many people looked to their monarchs as symbols of unity and peace, and it was certainly not in the interests of landowners to support movements that sought their dispossession. The Bourbons returned to France under Louis XVIII, and to Spain under Ferdinand VII. Austria and Prussia – the two largest states in a newly formed German Federation – were equally keen that the new forces of nationalism and liberalism be kept at bay. Tsar Alexander suggested that Russia, Austria and Prussia even come together in a Holy Alliance, ostensibly to promote Christianity. In reality, the objective was to suppress any liberal ideas of change to the existing system which might end in outbreaks of rebellion.

However, through the introduction of reforms, and by encouraging nationalist aspirations, Napoleon had unleashed forces of change that would become increasingly difficult to quash. In Western Europe, industrialisation was beginning to enrich a growing middle class, who were increasingly interested in the democratic ideas of the revolution, and less and less prepared to tolerate the tools of autocracy: secret police, arbitrary arrests and press censorship. Amongst other things, this class sought freedom of speech, the right to vote, representative government and a free economy – the French and American revolutions had shown that the status quo could be challenged.

In addition to the development of liberal thought, a new nationalist agenda emerged – predominantly in Eastern and

Central Europe – among ethnic groups living under the yoke of the Austrian, Ottoman and Russian empires. The ruling classes realised that these empires would disintegrate if such ideas were given any room to breathe. Their attempts to stifle them would ultimately lead to war.

Spain and Greece were the first to experience revolutionary activity in the 1820s. While the revolt in Spain was eventually put down – not without difficulty – a Greek independence movement succeeded in throwing off Ottoman domination in 1832.

France was next. Unhappy with press censorship, attempts to control parliament and the general illiberal tendencies of the French king, Charles X – who had inherited the crown from his brother, Louis XVIII – the Parisians rebelled. In 1830 Charles was forced to abdicate, and promptly fled to England, while his more moderate cousin, Louis-Philippe – who was descended from the brother of Louis XIV – was made king. That year revolution spread throughout Europe but failed to gain any real momentum. However, the old order equally failed to crush the new political ideologies entirely.

In 1848 there were further uprisings throughout Europe, with mixed results. The Hungarians – keen to be rid of their Habsburg masters – rebelled and were crushed. The Czechs demanded their own government, and the Austrians were driven out of northern Italy. In France, Louis-Philippe was expelled from France and the Second Republic was proclaimed. Napoleon's nephew, Louis-Napoleon Bonaparte, was elected president by popular vote. However, when he realised that standing for election more than once was forbidden by the constitution, he undertook a coup, dissolved the Second Republic and became a dictator. A year later, in 1852, he declared himself to be Emperor Napoleon III of the

Second French Empire – a position he would hold with some success until 1871, when France was defeated by Prussia in the Franco-Prussian war. Louis-Napoleon would eventually retire to England, where he died during an operation.

Britain narrowly managed to avoid revolution by making some last-minute concessions to the working class. Russia's turn would come later.

The Great Game in Central Asia

Despite Britain's increasing strength during the 19th century, the country still needed to defend its empire from encroaching powers. As the century progressed, Russia's interest in Central Asia – particularly the lands between Constantinople and India – increased. The area became a battleground where the two nations competed for spheres of influence in what came to be known as the 'Great Game'.

Russia's southerly expansion was the initial cause of concern: if they continued their southward progress through Afghanistan, it was feared they might be able to invade India via the Khyber Pass. Attempting to control the area, Britain invaded Afghanistan in 1839, but an insurrection there forced the army into ignominious retreat three years later, during which 16,000 soldiers and civilians were massacred. No attempt by a foreign power to rule Afghanistan has ever been successful.

A decade later, Russia caused further concern by invading two vassal states of the weakening Ottoman Empire in the Balkans, ostensibly to protect Eastern Orthodox Christians. This brought the Russians much closer to the Dardanelles and the nearby Bosphorus Strait, which linked the Mediterranean to the Black Sea. Once again, the British feared that this would give the Russians a sea route to India, thereby threatening

British control there. The destruction of a Turkish flotilla by the Russian Black Sea Fleet in 1854 gave Britain the pretext it needed to declare war. The French – keen to avenge their defeat at the hands of the Russians in 1812 – eagerly joined in.

And so began the Crimean War. The Russians were rapidly driven out of the territories they had occupied, and the Allies planned to follow this up with the quick capture of Sevastopol – the principal Russian naval base on the Black Sea – in present-day Ukraine. Underestimating the Russian defences, the war dragged on for a year until Sevastopol capitulated in 1855.

While the Allies won the war, the costs for both sides were immense, with the British and French losing up to 25,000 and 100,000 men respectively, and the Russians losing many multiples of this. The majority of deaths were from diseases such as typhus, cholera and dysentery, despite the best efforts of Florence Nightingale and her fellow nurses to look after the wounded and dying soldiers.

One consequence of Russia's defeat in the Crimea was a programme of reform and modernisation initiated by Tsar Alexander II, who came to the throne in 1855. While he is credited with the emancipation of the peasants in 1861, his reforms were haphazard and badly managed, ultimately leading to further unrest and to his assassination. Over the following years professional revolutionaries would play on the frustrations of the people, and would end up taking over the Russian state in the October Revolution of 1917.

The Opium Wars
While Europe underwent a period of industrialisation and revolutionary change, China experienced its own upheaval. The Portuguese had arrived in China already in 1517, but

the Ming Chinese had had no interest in learning from them, being convinced of China's superiority in all things. While not treated as equals, foreigners had been permitted to operate in Macau, a Chinese port from where they imported tea, silk, porcelain and other goods for which there was growing demand in Europe.

The Manchus were clear from the outset that all trade would be conducted on their terms via their own intermediaries, and that the Europeans should pay in silver for items they wished to purchase. However, the sheer quantity of purchases made by the British traders, and their general lack of success in persuading the Chinese to part with their own silver in exchange for foreign goods, began to affect the British balance of trade. Looking for a solution, the British realised that if their traders could exchange merchandise in India for raw materials, then exchange these raw materials for tea in China, they would stem the flow of silver from their treasury.

One of the products they obtained from India was opium, and to their joy, they found an insatiable demand for it in China. Used to relieve pain and reduce hunger, it was also employed recreationally. Within no time at all, a huge number of men under 40 living in the country's coastal regions were smoking opium, and by the late 1830s over 30,000 chests of it were being imported annually by various foreign powers. However, most of this was in fact smuggled into the country, as the Chinese government had recognised the social cost of the drug and banned it. In 1838, realising that their ban was being defied, the Qing government decreed that a death sentence would fall on anyone dealing in opium. When they realised a year later that this threat was not reducing the trade, government officials confiscated and then burned 20,000 chests of East India Company opium, scattering the ashes into the sea and offering no compensation to the traders.

For the British, the trade in opium and tea provided such significant revenues that this injury demanded a response. They sailed into the port of Canton with several warships, easily defeating the Chinese with the aid of their modern weaponry, and forcing the Chinese to open their ports to British trade. Furthermore, the Chinese were required to cede the island of Hong Kong, and to pay an indemnity for the opium they had destroyed. All this was in addition to accepting the distribution of an addictive drug throughout their land. This did not pass unnoticed in Britain, where a newly elected member of parliament, William Gladstone, wondered if there had even been 'a war more unjust in its origin, or a war more calculated to cover this country with permanent disgrace.'

The humiliation of the Opium War shattered China's false sense of superiority, and encouraged the rise of anti-Manchu sentiment that had been simmering beneath the surface since the end of the Ming dynasty in 1644. At the same time, China faced a huge population increase and suffered a number of natural calamities. The cumulative effect was increased impoverishment and unrest, ultimately providing the context for China's largest uprising and the bloodiest civil war in history.

Civil war in China (1851)

In 1851, a rebellion was launched by Hong Xiuquan, a village teacher who believed he was the younger brother of Jesus Christ, chosen by God to establish a heavenly kingdom upon earth, with himself as king. He would rid China of evil influences, including Confucians and Buddhists, replace the corrupt Manchu Qing dynasty, and restore China to its past greatness. Slavery, arranged marriages, opium smoking, foot binding and torture would all be abolished. The era of *Taiping*, or 'Great Peace', had begun.

Hong Xiuquan's version of Christianity had soon attracted over a million people, urged on by the hope of improved social conditions, land distribution and female equality. As a sign of rebellion, the men grew their hair long, and became known as the 'hairy rebels'. The civil war that followed lasted 14 years, claiming an estimated 20 million lives.

The rebellion almost toppled the Qing dynasty, whose attention was divided between the rebels and another opium war with the British and the French. However, it ultimately failed to achieve its objectives. The rebels had attacked Confucianism, which was still widely accepted in the country; they had alienated the wealthier classes by advocating radical reforms, and their leadership had been increasingly weakened by rivalries, resulting in the division of their forces. It did not help their cause that the Europeans refused to deal with them, unsure if their concessions would continue under a Taiping regime. Hong Xiuquan eventually killed himself.

Having lost control of many parts of China to local warlords following the death of Hong Xiuquan, the Qing government realised that they would not be able to keep control unless they embarked upon a programme of modernisation. Students were sent abroad to study Western ways, factories were established according to Western models and Western science was studied. However, the forces of conservatism proved to be too strong for any major change to be implemented.

By this stage, several European powers had observed China's weakness and seized the opportunity to gain territory at its expense. Russia was the first to take advantage, invading the north-eastern Chinese region of Manchuria in the 1850s. France colonised what is now Vietnam, and established a protectorate over present-day Cambodia in 1864; Britain gained control of Burma in 1885, incorporating it within India, and took Malaysia for good measure. The Netherlands took the East Indies. Japan, having been through its own modernisation programme, defeated China at the end of the century, forcing it to recognise Japanese interest in Korea and to cede Taiwan. For this and other reasons, the Chinese refer to the 19th century as the 'century of shame and humiliation'.

Revolution in India (1857)

Almost immediately after the Crimean War of 1855, the British were faced with a serious rebellion in India. Since the arrival of Europeans on the subcontinent, the interests of the local population had generally been subordinated to those of the newcomers. Christian missionaries had further challenged the local religions and way of life, unwittingly alienating a large percentage of the population. When the English army introduced rifle cartridges allegedly greased with pig and cow fat, this incensed Muslim and Hindu sentiments respectively, and resentments which had been simmering for decades came to a boil.

In 1857, a hundred years after the Battle of Plassey, the European-trained Indian armies mutinied in an effort to win back control of their country from the British. Pledging allegiance to the Mughal emperor, they murdered the British inhabitants of Delhi. After this, the uprising spread rapidly throughout India. Initially considerably alarmed, the British eventually managed to put down the rebellion because it lacked support and good leadership.

In 1858, as a direct result of the Indian mutiny, the British government abolished the Mughal dynasty which had by this time notionally ruled India for 300 years, although for the previous century the EIC had essentially controlled the subcontinent. The emperor was exiled to Burma, and the British government assumed the direct administration of India, a country with ten times its own population. British rule in India prevailed over a good two thirds of the country for the next 90 years, in what came to be known as 'the Raj' – a term derived from the Sanskrit word *raja*, which means 'king'.

The British government installed a viceroy and dissolved the East India Company. India was too valuable to Britain – both as a source of raw materials and as a substantial export market – to risk losing it. To establish beyond doubt who ruled the sub-continent, Queen Victoria was declared Empress of India in 1877.

How King Cotton led to Civil War in America (1861–1865)

The mid-19th century saw revolution and war in Europe, civil war in China and uprisings in India. America would also have its fair share of catastrophe in the form of a conflict that stemmed from a clash between the increasingly industrialised North, and the cotton- and slave-dependent South.

In Europe, more efficient machines had led to growing demand for both raw and finished cotton – demand that the markets struggled to meet. Sensing that huge profits could be had, many plantations in the deep South began to focus on growing cotton. Yet, while the cotton gin had solved the major problem of separating cotton from its sticky seeds, the cotton still needed to be picked. Plantation owners quickly calculated that the more pickers they had, the more land they could harvest and the richer they would become. As a result, demand for slaves, which had seen a decline in the late 18th century, skyrocketed. America's slave population almost doubled between 1810 and 1830, and by the 1850s slaves made up approximately half the population of the four main cotton states.

By 1840, the United States produced more cotton than any other country, and the value of its cotton exports exceeded that of all their other exports combined, effectively financing the country's early development. Cotton planters became some of the richest men in America. What they did not recognise, however, was that the emphasis on cotton and slavery in the South had led to a dangerous dependence on a one-crop economy, with few incentives to diversify. The opposite was true of the North – where the climate would not support cotton – which had become increasingly industrialised, and therefore less dependent on slaves. As slavery became less and less acceptable globally, the South found itself increasingly isolated, both nationally and internationally.

The slave trade with Africa had been abolished by the United Kingdom in 1807[88] and by the USA in 1808. Despite this, existing slaves had not actually been freed, and a lucrative internal trade had developed within the slave-owning states, as the ban on the importation of slaves had only made them more valuable. When Abraham Lincoln defeated a pro-slavery contender in the US presidential election in November 1860, it was the last straw for the South. While most Northerners were indifferent to the issue of emancipation – its proponents were highly vocal, but very much in the minority – it was a source of huge concern in the South. Led by South Carolina, seven

---

[88]   Though it would not be until 1834 that slavery was finally abolished in Britain's realm.

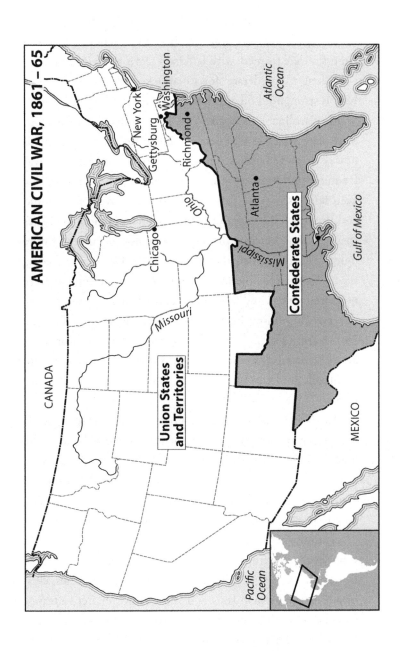

AMERICAN CIVIL WAR, 1861–65

CANADA

Union States
and Territories

Confederate States

MEXICO

Pacific
Ocean

Atlantic
Ocean

Gulf of Mexico

New York

Washington

Gettysburg

Richmond

Ohio

Atlanta

Chicago

Mississippi

Missouri

states left the Union, and in February 1861, a month before Lincoln gave his inaugural speech, the Confederate States of America were formed, with Jefferson Davis as their president.

When Confederate forces attacked Fort Sumter – a Union stronghold on an island in the harbour of Charleston, South Carolina – in April 1861, Lincoln had no choice but to declare war. He was determined to do everything in his power to prevent the country being torn asunder. This was far more important to him than the issue of slavery, and he even famously wrote that he would keep slavery if it would end the war. Emancipation was only one among many issues that saw him elected in the North, and most northerners were fighting for the principal of preserving the Union, not freeing slaves. Conversely, the majority of Confederate soldiers were not slaveholders, and were not necessarily fighting to preserve slavery. They most likely fought because they viewed the Union armies as invaders. In many ways, the Civil War was a battle between elites for economic power. Eleven states would eventually join the Confederacy, splitting the United States in two.

The North was in a stronger position from the start. It had a larger army and a population at least twice as large as the South's. It was also more industrialised – so could produce more war materials – and its superior transport infrastructure made resupplying its troops more straightforward. The North also controlled the navy, which proved significant in blockading the South and preventing the arrival of aid and supplies from Europe. Despite this, the Confederate general Robert E. Lee led the South to several initial victories, even invading the North in 1862 and 1863. However, Lee's advance ended in July of the same year at the bloody three-day battle at Gettysburg, Pennsylvania.

It was here, several months later, at the dedication of a new cemetery to honour the fallen, that Lincoln made his famous Gettysburg address – 'Government of the people, by the people, for the people' – which is regarded as one of the most significant speeches in American history. Ulysses S. Grant, the Union's most senior general – who later became the eighteenth US president – took command of the Union forces nine months after Gettysburg, and waged total war against the South until it was brought to its knees. The war officially ended on 9th April 1865, when Lee surrendered to Grant. Lincoln was assassinated five days later, at the age of 56, by a Southern sympathiser.

The Civil War was the most catastrophic event in American history: more than 600,000 Americans died, the majority through disease. This is a greater number than those who died in all other previous American wars combined, and exceeds the American losses in both the First and Second World Wars. Hundreds of thousands were also wounded. The South was destroyed, and the period of reconstruction that followed lasted over ten years. The effects of the economic devastation persisted much longer – well into the 20th century. The war did, however, end the debate over slavery.

The Expansion of America (1783–1867)

American independence had been accompanied by a huge growth in population, doubling to eight million between 1790 and 1814, and subsequently increasing to 23 million by 1850.

Much of this latter growth had come from an influx of Europeans seeking to escape Europe after 1815, attracted by the almost unlimited demand for labour in an expanding economy. A substantial number of Irish arrived in America from 1846 onwards, fleeing the terrible famine that occurred

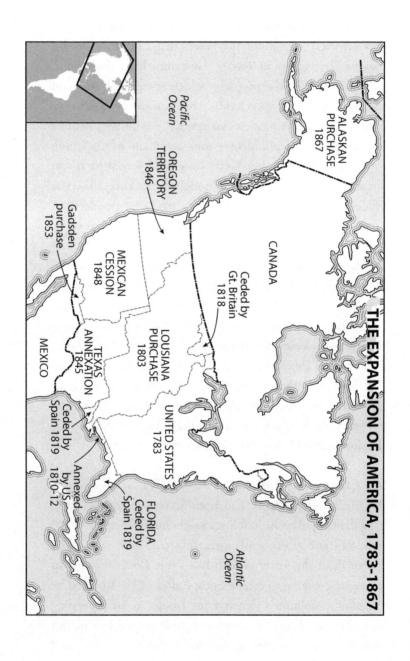

THE EXPANSION OF AMERICA, 1783-1867

ALASKAN PURCHASE 1867

Pacific Ocean

OREGON TERRITORY 1846

Gadsden purchase 1853

MEXICAN CESSION 1848

CANADA

Ceded by Gt. Britain 1818

MEXICO

TEXAS ANNEXATION 1845

LOUSIANA PURCHASE 1803

UNITED STATES 1783

Ceded by Spain 1819

Annexed by US 1810-12

FLORIDA Ceded by Spain 1819

Atlantic Ocean

between 1846 and 1851, caused by the devastation of Ireland's potato crop. This influx of people constituted an economic boom that led to the major westward expansion of the United States.

In 1803, under President Jefferson, America had purchased the entire two million square kilometres of the Louisiana territory from Napoleon – who had needed funds to finance his wars in Europe.[89] This area of land was roughly the size of Europe, and its purchase effectively doubled the size of America at the time. Further territory was gained by America's annexation of Texas in 1845. This caused a war with the Mexicans, who were then forced to concede California. Alaska, meanwhile, was bought from the Russians in 1867 for USD 7.2 million.[90] In 1898, after a ten-week war with Spain, the US also gained Cuba, Puerto Rico, Guam and the Philippines, although they never became US states.

The growth in its manufacturing industry and the production of cheap steel – a metal that is less expensive to produce, and both lighter and stronger than iron – allowed America to develop the railroads that were instrumental in opening its territory to trade and settlement. The railroad, the steamship and the telegraph reduced the cost and time of transportation and communication, and helped create a new market for American goods. By the end of the 19th century, the United States had become the largest and most competitive industrial nation in the world. In Europe, the flood of cheap American food led to falling European death rates and an increase in the population.

---

[89] Napoleon granted independence to Haiti in the Caribbean for the same reason.

[90] This equals roughly two cents per acre, which equates to about 30 cents in today's money.

New Nations: Italy, Austria-Hungary and Germany (1867–1871)

Increased population growth and surging nationalism in the 19th century saw Germany and Italy – long a patchwork of independent states – both become nations in their own right.

In 1848, much of Italy was controlled by foreign powers. A movement called the *risorgimento* aimed to unify Italy and restore it to its former glory. Several Italian states joined forces to oust Austria from its control of northern Italy, and the remaining states came under Italian control through diplomatic initiatives. Under the inspired leadership of the Camillo Cavour, Italy was united in 1870.

Germany's first step to unification had occurred in 1806, when 16 states left the Holy Roman Empire to create a new Germanic union – the Confederation of the Rhine – under the protection of Napoleon. A month later, Emperor Francis II had dissolved the Holy Roman Empire. At the Congress of Vienna in 1815, no attempt was made to restore the Empire, and the *Deutscher Bund* (the German Confederation) came into existence. Leadership initially fell to Austria, but unification was not high on its agenda and, as nationalism gained momentum, the states looked increasingly to the Prussian prime minister, Otto von Bismarck, for leadership.

A brilliant diplomat, Bismarck forced his reforms through the *Reichstag* (German parliament). Claiming that 'the fate of nations is not decided by speeches or votes, but by blood and iron', Bismarck dealt with any nation that sought to block his plans, notably beating the Austrian army in seven weeks. After unifying the Protestant northern German states under Prussian leadership, a victorious war against the French in 1871 allowed him to unify the remaining southern and Catholic German states. Thus began the Second Reich (the first having been the Holy Roman Empire) with King Wilhelm as their *Kaiser* (Caesar). A rapidly industrialising Germany then became the dominant military land power in Europe – possibly the most important political development on the continent between the revolutions of 1848 and the war of 1914.

Ousted from control of northern Italy and expelled from the German Federation following their defeat by Germany in 1866, the Austrians realised that it was in their best interests to strengthen their position by effecting a compromise with the largest national group in their empire: the Hungarians. A compromise was reached whereby a dual Austro-Hungarian monarchy came into being.[91] Franz Joseph was declared king of Hungary, and a separate parliament was established at Budapest, but the new empire would have a unified foreign policy, army and monetary system. In theory, this prevented the Austrian Empire from further disintegration. In reality, the preponderance of Slavs in the new empire would lead to trouble later on.

The Scramble for Africa (1880–1914)

Around this time, Europe became increasingly interested in the African interior. Before 1870, inland continental Africa had been largely ignored by the European powers, partly due to a simple lack of interest on their part, and partly due to a lack of resistance to tropical diseases – a weakness that saw Africa dubbed the 'White Man's Grave'. Any inroads they had made were predominantly in coastal towns, serving as either trading posts or re-fuelling stations, such as Cape Town. The interior was unknown, and Africa was also referred to as the 'Dark Continent' for that reason.

---

[91]   The new Austro-Hungarian Empire became the second largest country in Europe after the Russian Empire.

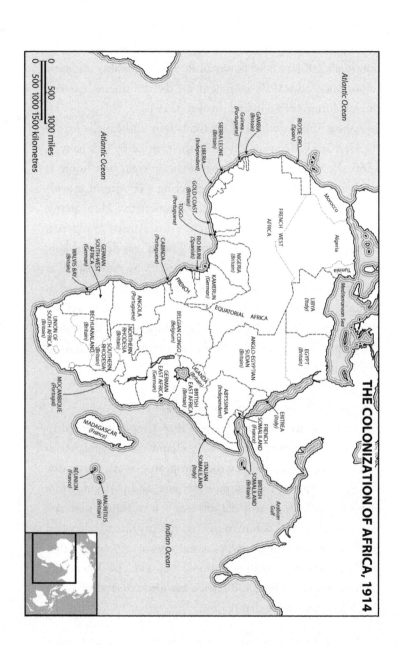

THE COLONIZATION OF AFRICA, 1914

Atlantic Ocean

Atlantic Ocean

Indian Ocean

Mediterranean Sea

Arabian Gulf

0 500 1000 miles
0 500 1000 1500 kilometres

RIO DE ORO
(Spain)

Morocco

Algeria

Tunisia

LIBYA
(Italy)

EGYPT
(Britain)

FRENCH WEST AFRICA

GAMBIA (Britain)
SIERRA LEONE (Britain)
Guinea (Portuguese)
LIBERIA (Independent)
GOLD COAST (Britain)
TOGO (Portuguese)
NIGERIA (Britain)
RIO MUNI (Spanish)
KAMERUN (German)

FRENCH EQUATORIAL AFRICA

CABINDA (Portuguese)

ANGLO-EGYPTIAN SUDAN (Britain)

ERITREA (Italy)

FRENCH SOMALILAND (France)

BRITISH SOMALILAND (Britain)

ITALIAN SOMALILAND (Italy)

ABYSSINIA (Independent)

UGANDA (Britain)
BRITISH EAST AFRICA (Britain)
GERMAN EAST AFRICA (German)

BELGIAN CONGO (Belgium)

ANGOLA (Portuguese)

NORTHERN RHODESIA (Britain)
SOUTHERN RHODESIA (Britain)

GERMAN SOUTH-WEST AFRICA (German)

WALVIS BAY (Britain)

BECHUANALAND (Britain)

UNION OF SOUTH AFRICA (Britain)

MOÇAMBIQUE (Portugal)

MADAGASCAR (France)

RÉUNION (France)

MAURITIUS (Britain)

However, as Europe industrialised, the need for raw materials to feed its factories grew, and more and more countries began to look to Africa as a new source of supplies, as well as a market into which they could sell their newly manufactured goods. The discovery of quinine, which gave some protection against malaria, together with the invention of new vaccines, contributed to lowering the death toll amongt Europeans and opened the country to further exploration. The final impetus was religious: European Christians saw a whole new continent waiting to receive the word of God.

Almost from the beginning, European nations competed aggressively for land. The French had lost territory (and pride) to the Germans in 1871 and their American empire no longer existed, thanks largely to Britain. They had also obtained a renewed taste for acquiring colonial possessions following their invasion of Algeria in 1830. The possibility of further expansion into Africa beckoned.

Britain was also seeking to expand its empire, which had been reduced since its American colonies had won independence. It was also made uneasy by Germany's rapid industrialisation and the aggressive policy of growth being pursued by Kaiser Wilhelm II. Sandwiched between the great powers of Europe, King Leopold II of Belgium saw this as his one chance to gain territory in a way that did not involve war, with greater territorial control bringing the promise of enhanced prestige. Leopold would go on to seize the Congo as his personal property. Portugal, Italy and numerous other countries also sought to get a foothold on the continent.

In 1882 the British invaded and occupied Egypt, concerned that instability there would affect the operation of the Suez Canal – built in 1869 – which significantly reduced the time and cost of travel to India. In attempting to protect Egypt from invasion, Britain also conquered the Sudan, to Egypt's south. With the strategic port of Cape Town in its hands since the beginning of the century, its route to India was now secure.

However, this unsurprisingly prompted a scramble by other European powers to gain territory in Africa. The speed at which they rushed into the continent encouraged Bismarck to call an international conference in Berlin to set the rules for dividing it up. No Africans were invited.

Within 20 years, most of the continent was under the control of one European power or another. Of all the African countries, only Abyssinia (later Ethiopia) and Liberia were never conquered by Europeans. The indigenous African peoples fared no better than the victims of previous European conquests: large numbers were enslaved and killed as the invaders raced to exploit the territory and its resources. As with the conquistadors, technological superiority compensated for vastly inferior numbers – this time, in the shape of the newly developed machine gun – in their attempt to tame what they considered an uncivilised land.

One of the overriding and lasting effects of European colonisation was the imposition of borders that cut across tribal boundaries. Disregarding existing tribal loyalties and fragmenting cultural and linguistic groups, the powers arbitrarily drew straight lines on a map in their haste to delineate their new colonies, thereby creating conflicts which continue to this day. It would take half a century or more before the African countries felt confident enough to rise up against their colonial masters and demand their independence.

The Technological Revolution
The westward growth of the United States took place in tandem with a technological revolution whose impact was

so great that it is sometimes called the Second Industrial Revolution.

In 1831 an English scientist, Michael Faraday, realised that an electric current could be produced by passing a magnet through a copper wire, thereby creating a potent new power source. He had invented the electric dynamo, upon which both the electric generator and electric motor are based.

Almost 40 years passed before a practical electric generator was built by the American serial inventor, Thomas Edison. For the first time in its history, humanity had a source of cheap and reliable power that could be generated almost anywhere. By 1879, Edison had developed a practical and long-lasting light bulb that changed the way in which people lived. Electricity was rapidly adopted all over the world, and its use was not limited to the home. Transportation and communication were also revolutionised by a flurry of inventions that appeared around the turn of the century. Alexander Bell invented the telephone in 1876; in 1885 Karl Benz produced the first gasoline-powered automobile, and in 1903 the Wright brothers took off in the first aeroplane. Advances in the applications of electricity were accompanied by huge developments in science, which helped unlock the secrets of physics and chemistry. Farming and healthcare benefited significantly from this, with the advent of more sophisticated fertilisers, pharmaceuticals and antiseptics.

The Rise of Japan (1895–1945)

By the turn of the 20th century, the USA and Germany were challenging Britain in the world market for industrial goods. Over in the East, a new power was emerging that was destined to take its place on the international stage: Japan.

Much like China, Japan had been closed to foreigners for many years, but the country was beginning to awaken, and with this awakening came growing imperial ambitions. The Tokugawa Shogunate oversaw a period of relative peace for the country, but a growth in population and a number of natural disasters in the 19th century led to increasing unrest. Having witnessed China's treatment by the West, the Japanese had sought to protect themselves against foreign interference by isolating themselves. Nevertheless, as had happened with China, trade was forced upon them, in this instance by the Americans.

In 1853 a heavily armed American fleet sailed into Tokyo Bay, and forced the country to abide by the trade terms it stipulated. The ignominy of these terms led directly to the collapse of 700 years of shogun rule, and to the emperor's restoration to the Japanese throne in 1868. The period came to be known as 'the Meiji restoration', or period of enlightened government. Despite attempts by traditional isolationists to prevent any change to the status quo, huge efforts were made to modernise and industrialise the country so that it could regain its independence from the Europeans and Americans.

Where China failed, Japan succeeded: universal conscription was introduced, with the Samurai replaced by a regularly conscripted army modelled on that of the Prussians. The British navy served as the model for the new Japan's new navy. Japanese scholars were sent abroad to study Western science; railways were built, and a European-style parliament was introduced. Class distinctions were abolished, education was improved and Western dress was adopted. Within a few decades, the country succeeded in turning itself from an agrarian and feudal society into a powerful industrialised nation – one which, to everybody's surprise, succeeded in defeating both China and Russia in two wars at the turn of the century.

In 1894, Meiji Japan defeated Qing China in a conflict of interests over Korea, which served as a buffer between the two nations. Following a battle that revealed China's much larger army to be woefully unsophisticated, Japan gained control of Taiwan and southern Manchuria. China was also forced to recognise Korea as an independent state. Japan would annex Korea in 1910, and rule it until 1945. Through China's defeat, Japan gained recognition as a rising world power.

Rebellion in China and the End of the Qing (1900–1911)

Increasing foreign intrusion into China by Western European powers had been accompanied by unwelcome missionary activity, the forced importation of opium and the acceptance of unequal treaties under which foreigners were accorded immunities from Chinese law. This combination of factors eventually led to a violent xenophobic and anti-Christian confrontation. The rebels were referred to as 'Boxers' by Western observers, from the closed fist that appeared on their banners. When the Qing threw their support behind the uprising in 1900, the Western powers acted decisively. The rebellion was suppressed by a Japanese-led 40,000-strong foreign army consisting of troops from Britain, the US, Germany, France, Russia, Italy and Austria. Tens of thousands of Boxers, Qing soldiers and civilians were massacred, and the last Qing emperor eventually abdicated in 1911. However, this was just the beginning of China's 20th-century misfortunes: more war would follow.

VII

THE 20TH CENTURY

The Bloodiest Century

Notwithstanding the rebellion in China, the 20th century began promisingly: there was general peace, growing prosperity, increasing contact between nations and a confidence that strong economic links would ultimately prevent a major war. Technological innovations were gradually improving the life of the masses, and the world was on the move. Yet within 50 years, two major wars and a great depression would bring down more than one world empire and change the balance of power. Even great progress is unable to change human nature and prevent man's inhumanity to man.

Oil and the Internal Combustion Engine

The 20th century could equally be called the century of oil. First discovered in sizeable quantities in the USA in 1859, oil rapidly became popular both as a lubricant for machines such as power-looms and train-engines, and for the ability of one of its by-products – kerosene – to fuel lamps. Prior to its discovery, gas and whale oil were used for lighting, but were generally unaffordable to all but the rich. It was the discovery that kerosene could be refined from oil, and that it could be produced inexpensively, that initiated a global search for oil.

When Thomas Edison discovered a new and revolutionary way of providing illumination through electricity in 1879, this 'new light' briefly threatened to eclipse kerosene as a means of lighting the home. The oil industry rapidly rebounded, however, when another of oil's by-products – gasoline – found a use in powering the internal combustion engine. When this was applied to the automobile in the 1890s, the car slowly started to replace the horse as the primary means of getting around, beginning a transportation revolution that still affects society today. Despite this, kerosene is still used in much of the developing world for lighting, cooking and heating.

The 20th century saw a major shift towards the use of oil in every sector imaginable, from powered flight through to agriculture, where oil-fuelled tractors and helped create the fertiliser used to increase crop yield. The resulting increase in food supply contributed directly to the growth in the world's population from roughly 1.6 billion in 1900 to 7.5 billion in 2017. The world's population is growing at a mind-boggling 100 million people per year, and the population is expected to reach c 9.5 billion by 2050.

Oil has not only fuelled armies but also played a large part in their strategies, including both the Japanese attack on Pearl Harbour and Hitler's eastward drive during the Second World War. Its discovery in the Middle East at the beginning of the 20th century transformed the politics of the area, directly causing more than one war, including the American-led response to Iraq's invasion of Kuwait in the 1990s. The application of oil has transformed human society to such an extent that today we would be lost without it.

Though we may live in a world of cheap energy, the consequences of our reliance both upon a non-renewable resource and the wealth it has generated may yet overwhelm us: we are becoming increasingly vulnerable to the disruption of oil supply and consequent sudden changes in price. What's more, the burning of fossil fuels has increased pollution to such an extent that climatologists inform us that, unless we take measures to reduce it, we face catastrophic consequences.

The Russo-Japanese War (1904)

At the turn of the century, Japan's military successes placed increasing power in the hands of militarists at the imperial court, whilst simultaneously fuelling their ambitions. When

Russia reneged upon an agreement to withdraw troops from southern Manchuria in 1904, these same militarists pushed for war. The outcome was a surprise attack by the Japanese navy on the Russian fleet at Port Arthur, on the east coast of China. Battles on both land and sea followed, in which the Japanese destroyed the Russian fleet and triumphed over the poorly led and badly reinforced Russian army.

Following the war, Russia agreed to evacuate southern Manchuria, which was restored to China, and to recognise Japan's control of Korea. By this stage, however, China's authority in the region was so negligible that it was not even invited to join Russia and Japan for the peace conference that followed.

The Japanese victory came as a shock to the world because Japan was the first Asian power in modern times to defeat a European one. Importantly, it showed that the Europeans were not invincible after all. The war also acted as one of the contributing factors to nationwide revolts in Russia in 1905, the outcome of which was a declaration of basic civil rights, and the creation of a Russian parliament – or *Duma* – in the same year.

The First World War or 'Great War' (1914–1918)

Over in Europe, growing nationalism caused the major powers to come into conflict once again, when nationalist movements, supported by Russia, threatened Austro–Hungarian interests in the Balkans. The assassination in June 1914 of the heir to the Austro-Hungarian Habsburg Empire – the Archduke Franz Ferdinand – and his wife by Serbian nationalists gave the Austrians the excuse they needed to crush Serbia and challenge Russian dominance in the area. With an unequivocal promise of support from Germany, they declared war. Russia's mobilisation of its forces made Germany nervous, however, so it put its own armed forces on notice. This made France anxious in its turn, and before long, France, Russia and Great Britain had allied themselves against the Central Powers of Germany, Austria-Hungary and the Ottoman Empire.

The war rapidly became one fought on two fronts: by the Germans against the French and British (plus dominions) in the west, and against Russia in the east. The British and German navies, meanwhile, battled it out on the seas. In 1915 there was an attempt to open up another front in Turkey by capturing Constantinople. This resulted in a massacre of predominantly Australian and New Zealand troops on the Gallipoli peninsula, in one of the war's greatest disasters for the Allies. Although they still officially deny it, the Turks used the cover of a news blackout to wipe out much of their Christian Armenian population, mainly on forced death marches in which large numbers died of starvation and exhaustion. It is estimated that between 1 million and 1.5 million Armenians and other ethnic minorities were killed or forced to flee between 1915 and 1923, in what was to be first of the 20th century's many genocides.

While the war was chiefly fought in Europe, it soon spread to Asia, the Middle East and Africa. In Asia, the Allies were supported by Japan; in the Middle East, the British sponsored Arab national movements opposing Ottoman domination in the area, only to cynically renege on any agreements at the end of the war. In the hope of enlisting the help of American Jews to persuade the US government to send more troops – probably overestimating the degree of their influence – the British also expressed their support for the creation of a

Jewish homeland in Palestine – a declaration[92] which they subsequently refused to honour. As with many peoples in the 20th century who found themselves pawns in global power games, the Palestinians were not consulted.

Everyone expected the war to be as short as the last war between France and Prussia (1870–71), but warfare had changed: modern weaponry simply led to mechanised slaughter and stalemate in the trenches. Over a million men died on the borders between France and Germany within the first year, with many forced to make doomed charges at enemy machine guns and barbed wire by generals whose tactical planning was based on 19th century models.

Just how badly the Germans had underestimated the Russians in the wake of the Russo-Japanese War became evident by 1915, as they had been forced to commit two thirds of their forces to the Eastern Front, even as the Western Front had become locked in a stalemate. Yet the Russian military was untrained and unprepared for the ferocity of the battle, and although on paper Russia's army was the largest in the world, by 1917 it was on the verge of collapse.

The Russian Revolution (1917)

Revolution in Russia broke out in Petrograd (formerly, and now once again, St Petersburg) in February 1917. Cold, hunger and general war-related weariness drove people to the streets demanding bread, and peace with Germany. The Empress Alexandra was unpopular: she was in thrall to the monk Rasputin[93] whom she claimed had healed her son, but who was a highly divisive figure, and her German blood made

---

[92]   The Balfour Declaration of 1917.

[93]   Rasputin was eventually murdered in 1916.

her suspect. When the tsar prevaricated in putting down the revolt, many troops joined the crowds, shooting at their own regiments. Finally understanding the severity of the situation, Nicholas II – the last tsar – abdicated in March 1917, thereby ending the 300-year-old Romanov Dynasty.

While workers' councils, or *soviets*, were set up to represent the masses, the temporary 'provisional government' that had inherited power continued to support the allied cause. This turned out to be a disastrous mistake. In April, the Germans pulled off a masterstroke by helping Vladimir Ulyanov (who used the pseudonym 'Lenin') to return from self-imposed exile in Switzerland to Russia. Leader of the majority 'Bolshevik' faction of the Russian Social Democrat Workers Party – as opposed to the Menshevik minority faction – since 1903, Lenin had been calling for the end of the 'imperialist and capitalist war' since it had begun. The Germans hoped that he would foment the unrest necessary to destabilise the Russian war effort, and even remove Russia from the war entirely. This would allow Germany to focus its resources on the Western Front.

The next six months saw a last-ditch summer offensive by the Russians which ended disastrously, with a flood of desertions and complete chaos, in which the government only just survived an attempted coup by the Commander-in-Chief of the army. Lenin was forced to flee to Finland, having been exposed as being in the pay of the Germans.

Yet the situation played into Lenin's hands. His call for peace, land, bread and transfer of power to the soviets became too strong for the exhausted population to resist. Returning to Russia again, this time in disguise, Lenin instigated an armed coup in October 1917. This was the final death-blow for the provisional government, and resulted in the creation of the world's first Marxist government. On the 8th of November 1917, Lenin was elected by the Russian Congress of Soviets as Chairman of the Council of People's Commissars. It was generally accepted that this Soviet government would not last long; nobody suspected the misery it would inflict on its people over the coming decades.

The new Soviet government immediately issued two decrees. The first – 'On Peace' – called for a negotiated end to the war and ordered Russian troops to cease all hostilities on the front. This had been part of a secret agreement reached between Lenin and the Germans in exchange for Lenin being returned to Russia. The second – 'On Land' – declared all land the property of the people – a good propaganda tool if ever there were one! They also nationalised the banks and repudiated all debt built up by the Romanovs. Hoping that workers throughout Europe would rise in support of their comrades in Russia, they sought to stall a further German advance by signing an armistice with Germany and Austria, pending a formal peace treaty.

However, the working class of Europe did not oblige. And so, desperate to end the war at any cost – especially after Germany continued its eastwards march – in March 1918 Russia was forced to accept a humiliating armistice. The terms of this treaty required Russia to give up Finland, Poland, the Baltic states, the Ukraine and Belarus. However, Lenin never had any intention of standing by the treaty – thereby setting an example of bad faith which later Soviet leaders would emulate – and Russia declared it null and void at the end of the war. It was also the last straw for anti-Bolshevik forces, which were let down by the Russian capitulation. The next three years witnessed a civil war that caused upwards of ten million casualties – more than the total number of deaths in the First World War.

The End of the Great War

The peace on the Eastern Front allowed a renewed offensive by the Germans on the Western front. However, Germany's decision to use unrestricted submarine warfare in the Atlantic proved as harmful to their cause as sending Lenin to Russia had proved helpful. It was this, together with Germany's attempts to entice Mexico into an alliance against the United States, that President Wilson cited as reasons for bringing America, with all its troops and resources, into the war on 6th April 1917. Unable to sustain the fight any longer, Germany surrendered, and peace finally came on 11th November 1918.

Of the 65 million men who had taken part in the war, over eight million were killed; up to 20 million were wounded – including hundreds of thousands blinded and crippled by chemical warfare – and several million others were captured and kept as prisoners of war. Worse still, in the final stages of the war, an influenza epidemic swept through already exhausted populations, killing an estimated 20 million people[94] worldwide – at least twice the number who had died in the War.[95] Named the 'Spanish Influenza' because the Spaniards had been one of the few nations not to censor information about it, the flu predominantly affected young healthy people, and proved virtually untreatable.

Following the war, the great powers met near Paris to deal with the aftermath and to ensure that Europe never

---

[94] Some people estimate that the Spanish flu killed up to 40 million people.

[95] This does not include the many millions who died of cholera, typhus, dysentery and other diseases after the war.

saw such devastation again. The Germans and the Russians were not invited to take part. The Treaty of Versailles that was signed in June 1919 is most memorable for the way in which Germany was treated. While all the interested parties wanted Germany punished for the damage it had caused, France specifically wanted to ensure that it would never be able to wage war on her again, and insisted on draconian and ruinous terms. Germany was ultimately deprived of some 13 percent of its 1914 territory, including the lands it had seized from France in 1870. It lost around six million of its citizens, and its overseas possessions were shared among the victorious powers. Additionally, its army was limited to a 100,000-strong defensive force, and the country was denied the right to possess aircraft, heavy weapons and submarines. On top of this, the French also forced Germany to pay huge war reparations of billions of gold marks. This humiliation and economic devastation created the instability that allowed Hitler and his Fascist minions to rise to prominence, and eventually take control of Germany.

The Treaty of Versailles included a clause that called for the creation of a multinational body – the League of Nations – designed to ensure peace in the future, and resolve any international disputes before they escalated into war. The Arab states created an equivalent organisation, the Arab League, to look after their own interests. One of the objectives of the League of Nations was to help territories liberated from German and Turkish rule to achieve self-determination. As a result, the multi-ethnic Austro-Hungarian and Ottoman empires were divided into smaller states along broadly linguistic lines – that is, according to the predominant languages spoken. Out of Austria-Hungary came Czechoslovakia, Yugoslavia, Hungary and a new Austrian Republic.[96]

In addition to being forced to grant independence to the Baltic states, the Soviet government had also been required to return to Poland the territory taken from it during the 18th century. Germany, likewise, had to return the land it had absorbed when the old Poland had been divided up between tsarist Russia, Habsburg Austria and an emergent Prussia, and had effectively disappeared from the map. At the end of the war, a new independent Polish Republic was recognised by the League of Nations. However, within 20 years, Poland would suffer both a brutal German invasion and a Soviet occupation, with the country once again being divided, and millions of Poles losing their lives.

The Ottoman Empire – previously tolerated as the lesser of two evils when the alternative was a regional power vacuum – was finally dismembered. Ignoring complaints by the Arabs – whose support for Britain against the Turks had been contingent upon the promise of independence – Iraq and Palestine were given to Britain, and Syria and Lebanon to France. To soften the blow, they were referred to as 'mandates' rather than colonies. Mustafa Kemal Pasha (later called Atatürk or 'Father of the Turks') abolished the Caliphate, and proclaimed the Turkish Republic in 1921. Wishing to turn Turkey into a modern secular republic, Atatürk embarked on a rapid modernisation programme, including the replacement of Sharia law by Western law, and of the Arabic alphabet by the Latin one.

---

[96]   Yugoslavia and Czechoslovakia would both be broken up by the end of the 20th century.

The Emancipation of Women

A positive outcome of the war was that the rights and status of women greatly improved, at least in the Western world. For most of history, the role of womankind in male-dominated societies had been to serve and obey their husbands, and produce children. Most professions had traditionally been closed to women and their education had been limited. Despite all the talk of justice and equality that drove the American and French Revolutions, women were still denied equal rights throughout the 19th century.

While this remains the case in many of the world's poorer countries today, from the mid-19th century, Europe and North America witnessed a growing movement advocating for women's rights which gradually led to increased education, employment and voting rights. In America, this movement developed from anti-slavery campaigns. Many of these had been led by women, who began to see parallels between slavery and female subjugation, as it seemed to them that women had no more political rights than slaves did. In Europe, the cultural, political and economic upheaval caused by the various revolutions helped challenge the status quo and increase demands for reform. The expansion of literacy and communications helped women verbalise and promote their aspirations. Frustrated by the slow pace of change, however, groups of women in England – known as the Suffragettes – resorted to violence in order to make their voices heard. The significance of their contributions to the war effort, however, only added momentum to cause, and it became impossible to justify not giving them the vote.[97] Although women had taken on traditionally male jobs during the Second World War and had subsequently remained in the workforce in large numbers, many advances in women's rights in the US only came about in the 1960s.

Many poorer, less-industrialised countries continue to resist moves towards greater female equality, and the exploitation of illiterate and uneducated women is still widespread in much of Africa, Asia, India and the Middle East. In these countries, boys – who are often considered a guarantee for economic security in old age – still regularly receive preferential treatment, whilst girls are often deprived of even basic rights. Whilst women are still regarded as second-class citizens, and, in many cases, little more than property, this will not change. Remarkably, women were only given the right to drive in Saudi Arabia in 2017.

The Russian Civil War (1917–1921)

Despite having sued for peace during the war, the Russians saw no respite for several years. So-called 'White' anti-Bolshevik forces (as opposed to 'Red' communist forces) – a curious alliance consisting of monarchists, Catholics, landowners and even moderate socialists – declared their intention of overthrowing the new atheist regime which had embarked upon a radical experiment to destroy an old society and create an entirely new one. Of course, these groups all had a vested interest in the old order, but while the Bolsheviks promised peace, prosperity, equality and an end to ethnic discrimination, what they in fact delivered was misery, class warfare and civil war.

---

[97] New Zealand became the first country to allow women to vote in 1893, the United Kingdom allowed women over 30 the vote in 1918, followed by all women over 21 in 1928. Lichtenstein was the last European country to give women the right to vote, only doing so in 1984. Women in Bahrain were only given the right to vote in 2001.

Even more committed to their cause after the communists executed the tsar and his family in 1918, the Whites received support – in both materials and manpower – from various nations keen to ensure that communism did not survive its infancy. These countries were acutely aware that the aim of the Soviets was to overthrow every other capitalist government.

In the end, the Bolsheviks won the civil war, but at a huge cost to both life and the economy. They were victorious partly through their success in holding the key cities; partly thanks to the efficacy of their war machine – run by their War Commissar, Leon Trotsky – and partly due to their ruthlessness, which instilled fear in the general population. But they also survived because the White forces were unable to unite against them.

Ironically, the Soviet state eventually became much more oppressive than the tsarist one that had preceded it. As the violence of the civil war died down, conditions began to improve only when Lenin relaxed his pure socialist economic policies. However, with his death in 1924, and with Stalin's rise to power, any vestiges of a market economy or civil rights disappeared. Creating a cult of personality in which he held absolute authority, Stalin brutally repressed any perceived or actual dissent. Those who challenged the regime were summarily executed – a policy which has characterised communist regimes ever since.

The Rise of Fascism and Totalitarianism

Following the war, Europe witnessed a period of inflation, unemployment and minor revolutionary activity, although the population was generally too tired to support any major uprising. The economies of Europe gradually recovered as a result of consumer demand, which grew rapidly after the deprivations of the war. Despite this, there was an undercurrent of fear in the business community that the communists might prey on unrest and come to power, seizing business assets in the process. This fear would lead to the growing power of ultranationalist groups throughout Europe.

In Italy, wealthy capitalists financed groups of thugs to terrorise communists and socialists who had instigated a wave of strikes. A new anti-democratic fascist movement gained momentum, advocating the use of harsh measures to solve the country's problems. Such was the support enjoyed by these fascists, that their leader, Benito Mussolini – a former school-teacher and journalist – successfully came to power and gradually imposed a dictatorship on the country.

In Germany, the Kaiser had abdicated after the war. The Weimar Republic that succeeded him attempted to print its way out of its war debts, only to unleash spectacular hyper-inflation, causing the financial ruin of millions of Germans. As a result, anyone promising order received a warm welcome.

One such was Adolf Hitler, an Austrian who had served in the First World War. He launched a virtual one-man campaign against the Treaty of Versailles, the harsh terms of which had incensed him and many Germans. In 1923, he proclaimed a revolution, and attempted to take over the Bavarian government in Munich, along with his army of followers. This failed uprising – for which he received a five-year jail term, of which he only served nine months – became known as the Beer Hall Putsch.

It was in jail that he wrote *Mein Kampf*, in which he blamed all the world's problems on the Jews, particularly communism and Germany's defeat in the war. Rather than allow German racial purity to be debased through contact with them – and the Slavs for that matter – they needed to be eliminated. Germany also needed living space, or *Lebensraum*, and he suggested it would find this by conquering Russia and the Slavic countries. Signatories of the Treaty of Versailles were traitors who had stabbed Germany in the back, and should be removed from power. Given the economic strife and hyperinflation in Germany, Hitler's beliefs found a ready audience, with the book selling five million copies before the beginning of the Second World War. Major industrialists, unsupportive of the government and concerned about the communist threat, bankrolled Hitler, erroneously assuming they could control him.

In Russia, the plight of the population deteriorated throughout the twenties and thirties. Before his death, Lenin had expressed misgivings about being succeeded by his Georgian colleague and General Secretary of the Communist Party, Joseph Stalin. Nevertheless, Stalin soon outmanoeuvred his rivals to lead the Soviet Union until his death in 1954. Trotsky was declared an enemy of the State, stripped of all authority and forced into exile. Many of the original revolutionaries who had resisted Stalin were executed or sentenced to imprisonment within the enormous system of slave-labour camps – the gulags.

As Stalin consolidated his power, he embarked on a course to catch up economically and industrially with the West. In 1928, he launched the first of his five-year plans, which involved the full-scale nationalisation of industry and the collectivisation of agriculture. At the time, the Soviet Union was underdeveloped and primarily agricultural, with very little industry. A world war, a civil war and a revolution – all in the space of five years – had stalled any possibility of progress. Stalin saw that the Soviet Union was 50 to 100 years behind the advanced industrialised countries; if it did not catch up within ten years, the country would be crushed. He therefore aimed to transform Russia into an industrialised state as quickly as possible.

However, the huge number of workers needed for such a goal required feeding, and the countryside struggled to provide enough food. Stalin and his allies thought they understood why: lots of small, inefficient farms with limited machinery could only produce so much. If all these little farms could be incorporated into huge communist ones, they reasoned, the benefits would be considerable. The farms would become more efficient, thereby improving agricultural activity; more grain would be provided to the cities; farm labourers would be freed up to work in the factories, and the extra grain produced could be sold internationally to fund more machinery. Most importantly, it would help the communists extend their power over the conservative and religious peasants, who were proving difficult to manage.

The main problem was that Stalin insisted on unrealistic production targets, so there was little surplus to feed the peasants. As the targets were set progressively higher, the peasants often received nothing, and starved. Understandably, this did little to incentivise production. Nor did the uprooting of peasants from their ancestral homes. Moreover, whilst the pre-revolutionary class of wealthier land-owning peasants – *Kulaks* – were already denounced as enemies of the state, those who had only recently received land as a result of the revolution, and were reluctant to return it, or its produce, to the state found themselves being placed in the same category.

When the Red Army was sent in to appropriate grain, wide-scale rebellion ensued, with people burning their crops and killing their livestock rather than hand it over to the regime. Those who opposed collectivisation were either arrested, sent to gulags or shot, and agricultural production was severely damaged as a result. The Ukraine suffered most: at least four million people died between 1932 and 1933, in a period that the Ukrainians commemorate under the name 'Holodomor' – their own version of the Holocaust.

In purely economic terms, Stalin's industrialisation was successful, with a 50 percent growth in industrial output during the first five-year plan, which included the building of hydro-electric dams, railways and canals. While some argue that Stalin's plans succeeded in providing the Soviet Union with the military capability to withstand Hitler's onslaught a decade or so later, others understandably argue that the ends could not possibly justify the means.

The Great Depression (1929–1932)

In October 1929, the roaring twenties came to an abrupt end when the New York Stock Market crashed. The economic depression that followed cast a long shadow over the 1930s. As stock values crashed and banks failed, Americans who had been investing and lending heavily in Europe called back their loans. This caused a ripple of bank failures around the world, and reduced the availability of cash for investment in businesses. As demand fell over the coming years, so did industrial production, and this, in turn, caused huge unemployment. As times grew tougher, people became ever readier to listen to anyone who could promise them a solution to their woes. To the socialists and communists, it looked as though the end of capitalism was nigh; to Adolf Hitler and his Nazi Party, it was the perfect opportunity to get into power.

As if the Soviet people had not suffered enough, Stalin's paranoia caused him to instigate a series of purges between 1934 and 1939, during which millions of Soviet citizens were either executed or sent to gulags, as 'enemies of the people'.

The purges were indiscriminate, touching anybody who could challenge Stalin's power. They hit the educated and professional classes, scientists, the intelligentsia, most of the country's top generals and the largest part of the Soviet officer corps.[98] However, the decimation of the officer class has been cited as a contributing factor in the Soviet Union's early losses to Hitler in the Second World War. Indifference to such a loss of life is, perhaps, unsurprising from a leader who supposedly claimed that 'One death is a tragedy, a million deaths is simply a statistic.'

Change in the East

If Europe witnessed significant change in the early 20th century, so too did Asia, and specifically China and Japan. China had changed little over the previous several hundred years, but there was growing discontent with foreign interference and, by association, with imperial rule. When the Qing emperor was overthrown in 1911, two millennia of imperial rule came to an end. Officially, the Republic of China had come into being, but in reality, the country was taken over by warlords. They would not be defeated until 1926, when a nationalist party – the Kuomintang – under the leadership of Chiang Kai-Shek, led a successful campaign against them and united the country.

When the nationalists needed cash to pay troops and buy arms, only the Soviet Union was ready to give them assistance. This aid was given on the understanding that they would cooperate with the communists, who had founded a Chinese Communist Party under Soviet supervision in 1919. However, Chiang had always been strongly opposed to communism,

---

[98] According to various estimates some 15,000 officers were shot during the Purges.

and shortly after uniting the country he carried out a purge against party members, during which tens of thousands of communists were executed.

Although the communists managed to rebuild support in the cities, where the disparity between rich and poor was greatest, in 1934 the nationalist military campaigns to defeat them eventually forced almost 90,000 communists to retreat. Their subsequent historic trek over 6,000 miles of land became known as 'The Long March'. It was during this journey that Mao Zedong became the unrivalled leader of the communists. However, over a third of their group died on the march. The nationalists had almost succeeded in wiping out the communist menace, and might have done so entirely had they not faced a much larger threat from the east: Japan.

The East at War (1931–1945)

The Japanese had held an economic interest in north-eastern China since the Sino- and Russo-Japanese wars at the turn of the century. The speed of Japan's economic growth, and its having sided with the Allies in the First World War, bought it a place at the Versailles negotiations as a major power in its own right. It was here that its territorial gains in China – many of which were made at the expense of the defeated Germans – were officially recognised.

Japan had expanded its interest in northern China throughout the 1920s, and had been defending its territory there with increasingly hostile military activity. This was driven by the need to feed a growing population: the limited arable land on the Japanese islands was offset by the plentiful natural resources in weak, sparsely populated neighbouring Manchuria. Japan's military strength made it confident that it could handle any uprising it might meet in these territories.

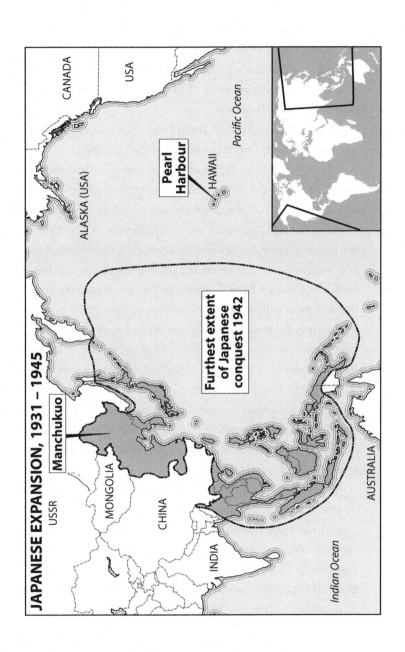

JAPANESE EXPANSION, 1931 – 1945

Manchukuo

USSR
MONGOLIA
CHINA
INDIA
AUSTRALIA

Indian Ocean

Furthest extent
of Japanese
conquest 1942

CANADA
USA
ALASKA (USA)

Pearl
Harbour

HAWAII

Pacific Ocean

When the Great Depression struck, Japan's trade suffered, as did its ability to pay for imported food. The protectionist trading policies introduced by Western governments only worsened the situation in Japan and increased military influence within its government.

In December 1931, using the threat of increased nationalistic activity and anti-Japanese sentiment in the region as an excuse, Japanese troops seized Manchuria. A puppet government was established, with the former Chinese emperor as head of state, and the territory was subsequently given the suitably Japanese name *Manchukuo*. While Hitler's notion of creating *Lebensraum* – 'living space' – in the east was still little more than a dream, the Japanese were implementing such a policy in China. Convinced that their country could become great only through self-sufficiency, it seemed obvious to the Japanese that they needed to expand their territory and gain access to natural resources. Moreover, having already invested heavily in Manchuria, they had no intention of losing this important asset. The Western powers, mired as they were in their own post-depression difficulties, could do little more than condemn Japan through the largely ineffectual League of Nations. Instead of leaving Manchuria, Japan simply withdrew from the League.

Many Chinese were angered and humiliated by the attitude of non-resistance taken by their government; Chiang Kai-Shek understood that the country was in no position to fight a superior army, and his priority was to destroy the communists first. Only then would he turn to face the Japanese. His generals eventually forced him to ally with the communists against the invader in an uneasy truce.[99]

---

[99] The truce lasted until 1941 when the nationalists turned on the communists.

In July 1937, using fighting between Chinese and Japanese troops as a pretext, Japan launched a full-scale invasion of China that started the second Sino-Japanese War, which laid the foundations for the Second World War in Asia. They easily overpowered the enemy troops, and within five months had captured half of the Chinese seaboard in a war of unprecedented brutality. In December 1937, Japanese troops entered the city of Nanking, committing some of the worst atrocities in the war: up to 300,000 men, women and children were butchered, in an orgy of rape and terror that easily matched the worst Nazi atrocities of later years. Above all, it showed their utter contempt and disrespect for the Chinese.

Millions of Chinese fled the Japanese terror by retreating inland, while Japan called for a Greater East Asia (consisting of Japan, Manchukuo, China and Southeast Asia) to be integrated politically and economically, under its own leadership. However, whilst Japan had thought the war against China would be over in three months, its troops became bogged down, forcing it to station an ever-larger number of troops there to keep order. Japan's investment in China provided a distinctly poor return in terms of resources, sucking in more than it gave back, preventing Japan from focusing its resources elsewhere and eventually forcing it to rely on the West for supplies.

The Second World War (1939–1945)

In Europe, meanwhile, by exploiting both the misery of the German people and general fear of communism, while promising jobs for all, Adolf Hitler's National Socialist (Nazi) party captured 18 percent of the popular vote in 1930. Three years later, he was appointed Chancellor of Germany, and by 1934 he had gained absolute power. The Third or 'Thousand Year' Reich had begun. The Third Reich's supposed predecessors – The First and Second Reichs – were retroactively defined by the Nazis for propaganda purposes – to legitimize their regime by suggesting a sort of continuity with a glorious past. Over the next few years, Hitler would terrorise his political opponents, eliminate any challenges to his power and, in direct contravention of the Treaty of Versailles, begin rearming Germany. Between 1936 and 1939, Hitler used the Spanish Civil War – which had ignited in 1936 following a military coup by the old order against a coalition of communist and socialist parties – as a testing ground for his new forces.[100]

In 1938, Hitler annexed German-speaking Austria and the German-speaking part of Czechoslovakia – the Sudetenland. Unprepared for war, Britain and France accepted Germany's actions, just as they had accepted Japan's invasion of Manchuria, in return for promises of peace. At the same time, they assured a nervous Poland that they would defend it in the event of a German invasion. By this stage, Hitler had already confirmed his plans for world domination: his ultimate goal was to regain Germany's pre-First World War territory by attacking Poland and striking at France, before turning to defeat the Soviet Union. To facilitate this strategy, and to maintain the safety of Germany's eastern borders while attacking France, he signed a non-aggression pact with the Soviet Union, in which the division of Poland was also agreed.

On 1st September 1939, Hitler invaded Poland. Standing by its promise of defence, Britain declared war on Germany, and other countries quickly followed suit. Within weeks, the Soviet Union attacked Poland from the east and annexed Finland and the Baltic States.

---

[100] General Francisco Franco, who represented the old order, became dictator and ruled Spain until his death in 1975.

The Katyn Massacre (1940)

Both Russia and Germany took many prisoners of war during their respective invasions of Poland. While substantial numbers died of starvation and disease, millions of others perished in forced labour and extermination camps. 21,857 prisoners of war were executed in 1940 on Stalin's orders, in a series of massacres known collectively as Katyn, from the name of the Russian forest where they took place. The victims were predominantly soldiers, but also university professors, physicians and lawyers. A Soviet Major-General – Vassiliy Blokhin – is said to have personally shot 7,000 of the prisoners using a German-made pistol renowned for its reliability. When the Germans discovered the mass graves in 1943 during their invasion of Russia, they were blamed by the Soviets for the massacre. The USSR only finally admitted, and condemned, Soviet responsibility for the act in 1990.

It was not until April 1940 that Hitler launched his major offensive on Europe. Denmark, Norway, Belgium, Luxembourg and the Netherlands capitulated in a matter of weeks, as did France. Some 225,000 British and 110,000 French troops were forced to evacuate via the port of Dunkirk. Hitler made his triumphal entrance into Paris on 14th June. Thereafter, France was divided in two, with a collaborationist Vichy government administering southern and eastern France, and Germany ruling the northern and western regions.

With France overwhelmed, Hitler planned to bomb Britain into submission and then invade it. The air war that followed, known as the Battle of Britain, was narrowly won thanks to the inspired leadership of the new prime minister, Winston Churchill – who had been appointed to the role only after Germany invaded Denmark – and to the bravery of a handful of Spitfire and Hurricane pilots. Hitler was forced to cancel his planned invasion of Britain.

Inspired by German successes, and desperate for his own empire in the Mediterranean and the Balkans, Mussolini declared war on Britain and France in June, and proceeded to invade Egypt and Greece in September and October. Italy also signed the Tripartite Act with Japan and Germany, effecting a military agreement to redivide the world between them.[101] The invasions were fiascos, however, and Mussolini's troops had to be rescued by the German Wehrmacht. Both territories were strategically important to Germany due to their access to oilfields, so Hitler could not afford for them to be taken by the Allies. While Greece was rapidly brought into submission, the battle for northern Africa lasted until May 1943.

The German intervention in Greece caused a three-month delay in plans to attack the Soviet Union. This delay would turn out to be critical, as the harsh Russian winter became a significant factor in slowing the German advance.

With most of Europe under German control, in June 1941 Hitler launched Operation Barbarossa, with the intention of forcing Russia into submission. Convinced that Germany only needed to kick in the door to 'send the whole rotten structure crumbling down', as he put it, and completely disregarding his non-aggression pact with Russia, Hitler sent a three-million-strong invasion force into the Soviet Union in the largest military operation in history.

Despite multiple warnings of imminent invasion, which Stalin dismissed as a campaign of false information, and despite the clear build-up of German troops on Russia's borders, Stalin was apparently taken completely by surprise: he was so shocked that he hesitated for an entire week before

---

[101] Germany, Japan and Italy were the largest of the Axis powers fighting against the Allied cause, of which the largest powers eventually included Britain, the USSR, the USA and China.

finally heeding his generals' urgent pleas that he take action. With the majority of his officer corps and generals executed in the purges, nobody had been willing to make any decisions without Stalin's approval; without specific orders to do so, Soviet troops did not return fire for hours. Consequently, a huge number of Soviet troops were captured in the first few weeks, most of whom died from starvation and disease.

Hitler's armies made remarkable progress, penetrating over 300km into Russian territory in the first five days, and the Luftwaffe reported destroying 2,000 Soviet aircraft in the first two days alone. Stalin's inability to grasp the situation on the ground, and his refusal to listen to the advice of his commanders, led to a number of devastating defeats for the Soviet forces in the first six months.

In the Ukraine, the Germans were welcomed as liberators from Stalin's terror. However, any initial goodwill was squandered by self-defeating German atrocities in the occupied territories. Jews were rounded up and shot, women raped, villages burned and civilians executed. In fact, for many Ukrainians there was little difference between their Soviet oppressors and the German invaders.

The War in the East

Hitler's armies reached the outskirts of Moscow in December 1941, before becoming bogged down by determined Soviet resistance and the arrival of the harsh Russian winter. With the Germans' advance finally checked, the world's attention turned to the east, where Japan – in a supposed 'war of self-defence' – attacked the American naval base at Pearl Harbour in Hawaii, killing over 2,200 Americans. Having perceived Japan's imperialism in China and the Pacific as a military threat, the Americans had forbidden the export of oil, iron and rubber to Japan in July 1941, as well as freezing all Japanese assets. Increasingly under the influence of its military, resource-poor Japan saw the USA as preventing it from fulfilling its destiny as Asia's leader. More importantly, with a thirsty war machine to feed, Japan saw no option but to seize the oil-rich Dutch East Indies, whose only protection was from token British forces and the US Pacific fleet.

The attack on Pearl Harbour brought the USA – led by President Franklin D. Roosevelt – into the war the next day, and, as in the First World War, the armed might and resources of the USA helped swing the war to the Allies. Up until this point, though it had provided them with aid, the US had stayed out of the conflict, having adopted an isolationist policy following the First World War. By mid-December, Japan had invaded much of Southeast Asia. The Japanese seized the Philippines from the USA; Indonesia from the Dutch; and Burma, Singapore and Malaya from the British with the intention of conquering China and uniting all East Asia under Japanese domination.

As Germany had in Europe, Japan rapidly won a series of victories in the east – and with equal brutality. In every territory the Japanese occupied, they carried out massacres and instigated forced labour and death marches in which millions died. Japan's victims were predominantly Chinese, Indonesians, Koreans and Filipinos, but also included Western prisoners of war, whose surrender was considered dishonourable.

America's entry into the war was followed by their victory over the Japanese fleet at the Battle of Midway in the summer of 1942. Undaunted, however, the Germans continued to make significant headway in Russia, threatening oil supplies from the Caucasus. Churchill became increasingly concerned that conquering the USSR would allow Hitler to dominate

Europe, and leave Germany free to attack Britain. As a result, he agreed to help the Soviets despite distrusting them entirely.

It was not until 1943 that the war eventually shifted decisively in favour of the Allies. The turning point came with the German defeat in the Russian city of Stalingrad (present-day Volgograd). This was the largest recorded land battle in history, which saw over one million deaths[102] and the first major defeat of Hitler's armies. The entire German Sixth Army was encircled, reduced, and forced to surrender en masse after Hitler refused to give an order to retreat.

After a series of running battles stretching across the North African desert – with victory alternating from one side to the other – the tide also turned in Africa, from which the Allies finally drove the Germans and the Italians in May 1943.

Capitalizing on their victory, the Allies launched an invasion of mainland Europe via southern Italy that summer. Mussolini was promptly deposed, arrested and imprisoned by the Italians, only to be rescued by German SS Commandos shortly afterwards. Meanwhile, the Italian government surrendered to the Allies in early September and changed sides, declaring war on Germany in October 1943. In June 1944, the Allies organised Operation Overlord, a massive combined invasion of northern France via the beaches of Normandy (D-Day).

Despite a few more offensives by the Axis powers (those powers who fought against the Allies), including a failed attack on the Western Front through the Ardennes Forest – popularly known as the battle of the Bulge – the writing was on the wall for the Germans. The final months of the war in Europe involved a race to Berlin between the Allies and the Russians; the Russian

---

[102] The Eastern Front saw approximately 75 percent of all German war casualties.

advance was notable for the savagery of the fighting, and the extremely brutal treatment of German civilians. On 30th April 1945, only two days after Mussolini had been captured and hanged by Italian partisans, Hitler killed himself. A week later Germany surrendered; Europe celebrated VE (Victory in Europe) Day the following day.

While the war in Europe was over, the War in Asia continued. The Americans gained the initiative in the Pacific and gradually forced the Japanese back, island by island, with terrible losses on both sides. In return for territorial gains, the Soviets were also persuaded to join the war against Japan. In July, the Americans had invaded Okinawa, the southernmost island of the Japanese archipelago. Poised to invade mainland Japan, and anticipating massive US and Japanese casualties, the US demanded that Japan surrender unconditionally or face destruction. The Japanese refused. On the 6th and 9th of August respectively, the Americans dropped atomic bombs on the cities of Hiroshima and Nagasaki, and Japan finally surrendered on 14th August 1945.

After the War

Some 60 million people died as a result of the Second World War. For the first time in history, civilian losses outnumbered military ones. The Soviet Union suffered more than any other nation, with some 20 million dead.[103] Poland lost the highest percentage of its population (approximately 16 percent) – six million people. Of these, half were Polish Jews (90 percent of its Jewish population) – half of the total estimated Jewish dead from the war.

---

[103] Roughly 750,000 Russians alone died in the 900- day siege of Leningrad between September 1941 and January 1944.

While it took a long time for the horrors of the Stalinist regime to come to light and be accepted, and while the atrocities of the Japanese had already been well publicised, the horrors of the Nazi concentration and death camps shocked the world. Slavs, gypsies, the mentally ill, and gay men and women had been added to the predominantly Jewish camp populations. Those who didn't die from exhaustion, starvation and exposure were murdered on an industrial scale in gas chambers and by other forms of execution in what came to be known as the Holocaust. It was these horrors that played a major role in the establishment by the United Nations (UN)[104] of the Jewish State of Israel on Palestinian land in 1948.

Japan was occupied by Allied forces – the first time in the nation's history that it had been occupied by a foreign power – and was forbidden ever again to possess an army. Its munitions were destroyed and its war industries were converted to civilian uses. Japan also lost all its overseas possessions, including Manchuria, which was returned to China, and Korea, which was divided into American and Soviet zones of occupation. The emperor of Japan only narrowly managed to avoid execution because the Americans believed that the administration of the country would be facilitated if he appeared to be cooperating with the occupying Allied powers. He was, however, deprived of his political power. Other leading military men were not so lucky, and were executed for war crimes following quick trials. Japan remained occupied, predominantly by the Americans, until 1952 when the country became a parliamentary democracy.

---

[104] The United Nations had been founded in June 1945 with the objective of managing the peaceful settlement of disputes after the catastrophe of World War II. All major decisions were to be taken by the victorious Great Powers of the United States, the Soviet Union, Great Britain, France and China.

The Arab-Israeli Conflict

The establishment of the Jewish State of Israel in 1948 was met by a joint military offensive of Arab countries including Syria, Egypt, Iraq and Lebanon. However, Israel defended itself successfully and emerged in a stronger position than before, increasing the territory it had been given by a third. During this conflict, some 500,000 Palestinians were forcibly expelled or fled in panic, in what has since become known as the *Nakba* – the Arabic word for catastrophe. The UN partition plan proved to be a terrible failure, laying the foundation for repeated conflicts in the Middle East such as the Arab-Israeli wars of 1967 and 1973. The latter of these led to a global increase in oil prices, contributing directly to a severe world recession.

The Palestinian refugee problem has still not been resolved, with some four million currently living around the world and unable to return home. Many believe that the inability to solve this thorny issue is a major factor in the global increase in Islamic terrorist acts over recent decades. Conflict between the Arabs and the State of Israel – which was, and still is, unwaveringly supported by the United States – has dominated international politics for much of the post-war period.

The New World Order

Two major and often interlinked themes dominated global history between the end of the Second World War and the turn of the 21st century. The first was the ideological Cold War between Western liberal democracy and communism – a battle in which Europe saw its position at the centre of the world replaced by the USA and the USSR – and the second was the efforts of the colonies of the great powers to gain independence.

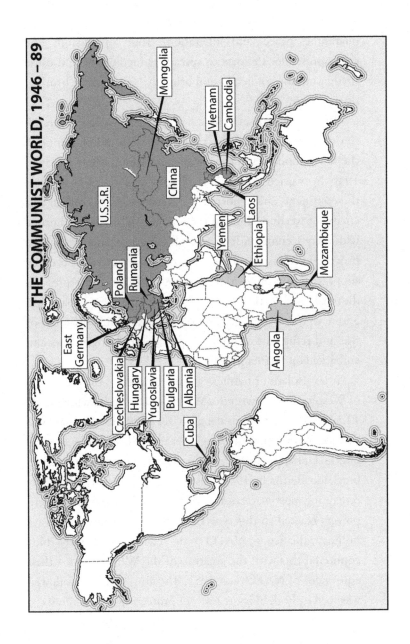

THE COMMUNIST WORLD, 1946 – 89

East Germany
Czecheslovakia
Hungary
Yugoslavia
Bulgaria
Albania
Cuba
Poland
Rumania
U.S.S.R.
Mongolia
China
Vietnam
Cambodia
Laos
Yemen
Ethiopia
Mozambique
Angola

The defeat of fascism and Nazism did not, unfortunately, guarantee peace and liberation from oppression: the communist bloc's efforts to spread its ideology would cause further millions of deaths and bring the world to the brink of nuclear war.

The circumstances of war had forced Winston Churchill to deal with Stalin, much against his will, and he was one of the few to understand the danger of communism. Already in 1946, he warned that an 'iron curtain' was descending across the continent, and exhorted Western powers to contain this enemy of freedom. During the war, much of Eastern Europe had already come under Soviet domination, and the Soviets proceeded to install puppet communist regimes that brutally suppressed any opposition. Neither did fear and repression diminish within the Soviet Union itself, where a paranoid Stalin, tightening his grip, sent forcibly returned prisoners of war and refugees to labour camps, deported Soviet Jews and embarked on further purges.

A less isolationist America funded much of the rebuilding of Western Europe with the Marshall Plan, under which USD 12.5 billion of aid (equivalent to over $100 billion today) was distributed over the following six years, leading to an economic boom. Unhappy with this, the Soviet Union attempted to blockade Berlin in 1948, destroying in one fell swoop any remaining post-war trust between the two blocs. Western powers reacted to this new situation by creating a defensive military alliance – NATO – in 1949. The Eastern bloc countered this with the creation of the Warsaw Pact – their equivalent of NATO – in 1955. The arms race that followed was seen by both blocs as a way of protecting their interests.

Unable or unwilling to attack each other directly, the two new global powers of the USA and the USSR engaged in proxy wars, bolstering 'friendly' regimes as a way of increasing their global influence. Military conflicts in China, Korea and Vietnam, among others, were all born as a direct result of this support.

Paradoxically, it was Japan and Germany – the aggressor countries, which had previously both faced total destruction – that ultimately benefited most in the post-war period. Prevented from spending money on arms by the victors, they both invested in industry and in rebuilding their infrastructure, and this led to an economic boom. Germany's growth in the 1950s was so strong that its economy became the strongest in Europe. No wonder the Germans called it a *wirtshaftswunder* – 'economic miracle'.

In the meantime, America's attempt to create an ally in the Far East, to counter the growth of communism in neighbouring China, meant that Japan benefited from American post-war investment. Japan grew to be the second largest economy in the world until it was overtaken by China in the 21st century.

Revolution in China (1949)

Soon after the defeat of Japan, China's civil war resumed between the communists, supported by the Soviet Union, and the nationalists, supported by the USA. Despite initial nationalist successes, the communists rapidly gained the upper hand, forcing Chiang Kai-Shek to resign in January 1949. He retreated with his government and two million people to the island of Taiwan, which was proclaimed the temporary capital of China. His nationalist government was recognised by most Western nations as the legitimate government of China for many decades.

In October 1949, Chairman Mao declared that 'the Chinese people have stood up!' and proclaimed the People's

Republic of China in opposition to the Taiwan-based Republic of China. A few months later, China and the Soviet Union signed a Sino-Soviet treaty of alliance. Almost half the world's landmass was now under communist rule, with China becoming the largest communist state in the world. The people of both countries would suffer tremendously.

No sooner had the communists taken power in China than they supported an attempt by communist North Korea to occupy the democratic South, in a war that lasted until 1953 and caused four million deaths. South Korea only managed to defend itself through Western support. A decade or so later, China would also give significant support to communist North Vietnam in its battle to unite with the south.

De-Stalinisation and the Space Race

In Russia, Stalin's long rule of terror finally came to an end with his death in 1953. He had suffered a stroke, but was not attended to for several hours. Whether this was due to fear of disturbing him, or through wilful neglect, is not known, but the world breathed a sigh of relief. Three years later his successor, Nikita Khrushchev, first privately and then publicly criticized Stalin's tyrannical rule, condemning the crimes committed under his leadership and releasing a number of political prisoners. Many Russians, still brainwashed by Stalin's propaganda machine despite the fact that so many of them had suffered so terribly under Stalin's rule, considered it a betrayal.

Khrushchev also instigated a policy of 'peaceful co-existence' with the West, to allow the Soviet Union to develop its economy without having to dedicate so much of its budget to defence. While this policy was welcomed warmly by Eastern European satellite countries, the thaw only went so far: when, in 1956, Hungary called for a multi-party political system and withdrawal from the Warsaw Pact, Soviet troops invaded.

In Germany, the flight of East German citizens to Western Germany was stemmed by the erection of the Berlin Wall in 1961. In the following decades, while some 5,000 East Germans successfully managed to escape to the West, at least 170 were shot in the attempt. In 1968, when Czechoslovakia tried to initiate some political liberalisation – a period known as the 'Prague Spring' – the country was occupied by Soviet troops.

The Soviet Union's 1957 launch of Sputnik 1, the world's first satellite, came as a shock to the United States, bringing fear that the same technology could be used to hit targets in America. Thus began a space race, which saw the Soviet Union send the first man into space (Yuri Gagarin) in 1961.[105] The USA landed the first men on the moon (Neil Armstrong and Buzz Aldrin) eight years later in July 1969 – a mere 66 years after the Wright brothers had managed to get the first plane into the air.

In the increasingly tense atmosphere that followed Gagarin's mission, the world came to the brink of nuclear war: in 1962, Khrushchev attempted to install nuclear missiles in Cuba, in what became known as the Cuban Missile Crisis. The situation was defused only when President John F. Kennedy agreed to remove (obsolete) US missiles from Turkey, in exchange for the Soviets removing their missiles from Cuba.

The Great Leap Forward in China (1958–1962)

After the launch of Sputnik 1, Khrushchev boasted that the Soviet Union would surpass the USA in economic production within 15 years. Returning from Moscow immediately

---

[105] The Soviet Union launched a dog into space the month after.

following the launch, and not wishing to be outdone by the Soviet Union, Mao declared that China would catch up with – and ultimately overtake – the economic production of Britain within the same time-scale. He called it the 'Great Leap Forward'. His attempt to achieve this ended with arguably the greatest catastrophe the country has ever known, and caused the death – predominantly from hunger – of tens of millions of people.[106]

Ignoring the terrible hardships, not to mention the millions of Russian and Ukrainian deaths inflicted by Stalin's five-year plans of the early 1930s, Mao instigated a programme of rapid industrialisation and collectivisation. In an attempt to meet unachievable targets, the entire population was mobilised to set up backyard furnaces. Pots, pans and farming implements were just some of the metal objects sacrificed in the drive for steel production, although the results were always of questionable quality. To run the furnaces, forests were cut down and houses destroyed. Millions were pushed into communes of collectivised farm holdings, whilst millions of others were mobilised to take part in massive, and generally unsuccessful, countrywide irrigation projects. This merely resulted in a shortage of agricultural workers to tend the crops and a lack of implements with which to gather them. With targets continuously revised upwards, they became less and less possible to achieve. This led to rice husks being filled with water to increase their weight, whilst crops were often left to rot due to woefully inadequate infrastructure and disorganisation. Worse still, in order to give the impression that China was close to becoming a communist paradise (but also to raise the funds necessary to buy foreign machinery), what

---

[106] Estimated at 45 million people by Frank Dikötter in his book, *Mao's Great Famine*.

little grain was collected was often exported in an attempt to hide the massive shortfall. Significant quantities of grain were also donated to communist regimes elsewhere in the world.

Such spectacular mismanagement led to severe grain shortages, resulting in mass starvation throughout the country. The majority of the livestock that was not exported often starved to death alongside the human population. Cotton did not escape the export quotas, so the people were reduced to wearing rags. Despite these obvious problems, the Chinese Communists adopted the Stalinist approach to criticism, imprisoning or executing any dissenters, and blaming any shortcomings of 'The Great Leap Forward' on counter-revolutionary activity. Mao seems to have shared Stalin's and Hitler's disregard for human life, supposedly responding to these problems by stating, 'When there is not enough to eat, people starve to death. It is better to let half the people die so that the other half can eat their fill.'

As if the population had not suffered enough, in an attempt to reassert his authority, in 1966 Mao launched the Cultural Revolution. Bands of young revolutionaries – the Red Guard – were encouraged to roam the country destroying the 'Four Olds': old customs, old habits, old culture and old thinking. Older authority figures were verbally and physically attacked, and the Communist Party was purged. Millions of 'counter-revolutionaries' were subsequently sent to labour camps in the countryside.

Political and ideological relations between China and the Soviet Union had been degenerating before the Cultural Revolution, as Beijing began to supplant Moscow as the ideological leader of the world communist movement, and continued to worsen. Mao had supported Stalin ideologically and politically, despite having been treated by him as an inferior younger brother, but had now become concerned both by Khrushchev's attempts at de-Stalinisation and his advocacy of peaceful co-existence between communist and capitalist nations. Mao saw this as a betrayal of Marxism and a clear retreat from the struggle to achieve global communism. In 1960, the Soviet side withdrew its aid to China in what became known as the Sino-Soviet split, and in 1969 the two countries even saw military conflict on their borders. Sino-Soviet relations only warmed again in the 1980s, after Mao's death.

Vietnam and Cambodia

In the meantime, China had been lending significant support to communist North Vietnam, which was attempting to unify with the South by force. There was little support for this in South Vietnam, which had large pockets of Catholics and non-Vietnamese minorities. Concerned that communism in Vietnam would spread to other parts of the world, the United States and other anti-communist nations supported the democratic South both financially and militarily. US support escalated over the following eight years, leading to a full-blown undeclared war by 1965, when the US president – Lyndon B. Johnson – committed over half a million troops to aid South Vietnam. The war lasted until the US negotiated a cease-fire and withdrew its military forces in 1975. While America lost some 60,000 troops – including 2,000 'Missing in action' – the Vietnamese, both in the South and in the North, lost at least twenty times that many.

Neighbouring Cambodia also suffered terribly as a result of the war. By 1969 the USA had started to bomb Vietcong supply routes there, killing 500,000 Cambodian civilians, and driving thousands more either to join the Khmer Rouge – a weak communist guerrilla force at the time – or to flee to the cities. The Khmer Rouge eventually seized power in 1975, invading the capital city of Phnom Penh. They forced the populations of entire cities into the countryside to a regime of forced labour in collective farms.

Over the following four years, approximately two million people – or roughly one third of the country – died from starvation, overwork and execution during an attempt by the Khmer Rouge's leader, Pol Pot, and his henchmen to turn Cambodia into a pure agrarian society. Over a million were the victims of state-sponsored genocide in the execution grounds that became known as Killing Fields.

The widespread and systematic brutality adopted by the Khmer Rouge easily matched and perhaps even exceeded the worst brutality of the Nazi SS, the Soviets, and the Japanese during the Second World War. Pol Pot survived and lived until 1998; some of his henchmen were finally brought to justice only in 2011.

The Microchip and the Digital Revolution

Alongside the steam engine and electricity, the invention of the microchip in the middle of the 20th century must surely be reckoned as one of the most important innovations of all time, in terms of revolutionising the way in which we live and work. Calculators, computers, the Internet and mobile phones all exist thanks to the microchip, and the world would move at a considerably slower pace without them. What used to take weeks to communicate now takes seconds. Whether we control technology or technology controls us is another question, however.

The Communist Holocaust (1917–1991)

Communist regimes were responsible for a greater number of deaths than any other movement in history, with torture, mass execution, starvation, terror, forced labour camps and murder all justified in the name of building a communist utopia. In their efforts to bring about the greatest human happiness, communists have brought about unprecedented human suffering. The death-toll is staggering: if we include the estimated 50 million deaths that occurred through famine – the result of misguided agricultural strategy or deliberate government policies – it is believed that communism was the direct cause of over 100 million deaths in the 20th century or, to put it into perspective, more than those killed in all the century's wars, revolutions and conflicts combined.

The Chinese and Soviet communists executed the largest numbers of people, while the Cambodian communists murdered the largest percentage of their own population. Three of the four worst dictators the world has known – judged in terms of the number of deaths caused – have been communist: Mao, Stalin, and Pol Pot. Communist regimes still in existence today include the morally bankrupt Democratic People's Republic of Korea (North Korea) – which continues to run a network of forced labour camps – China, Cuba, Vietnam and Laos. Even those which have experienced recent liberalisation are nevertheless characterised by lack of democratic freedoms, and frequently appalling human rights abuses.

Decolonisation: The End of Overseas Empires

The other major global movement since the end of the Second World War has been the decolonisation of much of the world. British India – which had been under British control for 90 years by the end of the war – was one of the first to go. Mohandas 'Mahatma' Gandhi, a British-educated lawyer, became the figurehead of a peaceful resistance movement, encouraging Hindus and Muslims to unify in their fight for independence and self-government. Britain had invested significantly in large-scale infrastructure projects in India, and the sub-continent was both a substantial market for British goods and a supplier of a large low-cost standing army. Hence, it initially responded negatively by imprisoning Gandhi and his colleagues, failing to appreciate that this would only contribute to the success of the independence movement in the long term.

Gandhi was less successful in healing the divisions between India's Hindu and Muslim populations, which clashed with increasing frequency. It soon became clear to everyone that independence would only be successful if Indian Muslims were given their own territory. In August 1947, following almost 350 years of colonial presence in India, two new nations came into being: a predominantly Hindu and Sikh India, and a predominantly Muslim Pakistan. However, what should have been a joyful occasion was marred through sectarian violence, and by the death of hundreds of thousands from both sides as people settled into their new countries.

In Asia, many colonies were initially returned to their former rulers following the war, and only obtained independence much later. France, which had fought to build a colonial empire since Napoleon's defeat, granted independence to Cambodia and Laos after the Second World War, but it tried particularly hard to hold on to other colonial territories. Sending an army into Vietnam only ended in decisive defeated there in 1954 at Dien Bien Phu. Then, having failed to learn its lesson, it fought a bloody, decade-long war against insurgents in Algeria, from which Charles de Gaulle was ultimately forced to withdraw the defeated French armies in disgrace in 1962.

Algeria was followed by other African countries, encouraged by a growing and global independence movement to demand self-rule. Many countries were offered support by the communist bloc, which hoped to gain influence in the region. In South Africa, a predominantly white government refused to give the majority black population any say in the running of the country. This regime of apartheid attracted international opprobrium that eventually resulted in an economic boycott. This isolation played a large part in forcing change in South Africa, alongside patient, non-violent resistance led by the imprisoned Nelson Mandela. His inspired leadership subsequently created a government that allowed for transition from apartheid to peaceful co-existence rather than bloody civil war, years of instability and worsening poverty, which is the more common result of such transitions.

When required, Western nations would come together to defend their strategic interests. This happened when French, British and Israeli troops invaded Egypt, whose president, Colonel Nasser, intended to nationalise the Suez Canal – the canal that links the Mediterranean Sea to the Red Sea. Whilst militarily successful, the action was a political disaster, particularly for Britain. They also colluded in the Middle East where, in 1953, the British and Americans arranged for the hugely popular and democratically elected Iranian premier, Mohammad Mossadegh, to be replaced by the previously deposed Shah, after Mossadegh nationalised the Anglo-Iranian oil company. The Shah was eventually overthrown in 1979, to be replaced by a fundamentalist Shia Muslim government which continues to be a major supporter of Middle Eastern terrorist groups.

By 1980, few Western colonies remained. Much of Eastern Europe, on the other hand – where wartime German subjugation had been replaced by post-war communist subjugation – had to wait until the dissolution of the Soviet Empire before it would be free again.

The Collapse of the Soviet Union (1991)

The collapse of the Soviet Union was inevitable, as it had become both morally and financially bankrupt through the continued repression of its people and its attempts to match the USA in military spending. Its shortcomings were represented by a stagnating economy, a shortage of goods and general disillusionment with the regime.

To revive the economy, the Russian premier Mikhail Gorbachev – a committed communist – called for a programme of market-oriented economic reforms (*Perestroika*) and openness (*Glasnost*) in the mid-1980s, probably not suspecting that this would lead to the dissolution of the USSR within six years. Despite growing economic problems for which there was no quick fix, Gorbachev's popularity soared, thanks largely to the fact that people became less fearful of speaking openly. He had let the genie out of the bottle.

The collapse of the communist Eastern bloc was sudden and relatively bloodless as revolutions go. Poland became the first non-communist government in Eastern Europe. In Czechoslovakia, a human rights campaigner, Vaclav Havel, was elected president. In October 1989, the East German leader, Erich Honecker, was pressed into resigning and East Germany opened its borders. Thousands of Eastern Europeans fled to the West, unsure of how long the border would remain open. Within a month the hated Berlin Wall had been torn down, and Germany was unified the following year.

In August 1991, Soviet government hardliners – unhappy about these changes, and totally out of touch with the people they ruled – attempted a coup. However, massive demonstrations ensued, led by the Mayor of Moscow, Boris Yeltsin, and the barricading of the Russian parliament by the people brought the coup to an end within days. Having had a small taste of freedom, the people understandably had no intention of returning to the old system. On Christmas Day 1991, Gorbachev resigned as Soviet president, and the USSR was formally dissolved, giving way to 15 independent countries. The Russians had lost the Cold War. A single anecdote encapsulates the situation: 'the end was almost too perfect: Gorbachev's Soviet pen would not write and he had to borrow one from a CNN cameraman.'[107]

For the new nations that sprang up after the collapse of the communist bloc, life was not as rosy as they had expected it to be: unprepared for independence, and with little experience of managing a free-market economy, they struggled under tough economic conditions and major increases in crime. Almost immediately, Yugoslavia fell apart in a brutal and bloody civil war. Territorial and ethnic conflict intensified elsewhere, and terrorism became increasingly common.

The Cold War had acted as a lid on simmering disputes, as order had come about 'through the superpower dominance of two blocs and superpower influence in the third world.'[108] Many nations now acquired highly sophisticated weapons and even nuclear capability, which some nations saw as the only effective means of challenging powers whose might couldn't be defeated on a conventional battlefield. Indeed, when it was suggested that oil-rich but politically unstable Iraq might be developing nuclear weapons, the USA used it as an excuse for invasion in 2003.

---

[107] *Why the West Rules for Now* by Ian Morris, Profile Books.

[108] *The Clash of Civilisations* by Samuel Huntington.

The Pendulum Turns: Europe Loses its Dominance

After the Second World War, Europe 'finally achieved peacefully what the Habsburgs, Bourbons, Napoleon and Hitler failed to achieve through violence'.[109] Yet by the end of the 20th century, Western Europe could already see its dominance in world affairs beginning to fade. Despite coming together in 1957 under the banner of the European Economic Community, and 40-odd years later under a common currency, European economies have been in decline. Competition with the dynamic growth witnessed in other parts of the world has become increasingly difficult, specifically with China, a country which is regaining the place it formerly occupied in the world. The gravitational centre of world power seems to be slowly shifting from the West back to the East.

Economic growth in Asia was the success story for much of the 1990s, to the extent that the economies of Hong Kong, Singapore, South Korea and Taiwan were dubbed the 'Asian Tigers'. Growth then moved to China and to other countries in Asia. Whilst for many Asian countries, economic growth saw capitalism and democracy flourishing in tandem, China managed to successfully introduce a mixture of capitalism and authoritarianism that created the fastest-growing economy in the world. Indeed, inexpensive Chinese labour reduced the cost of living in the rest of the world, and contributed substantially to what little economic growth occurred in Western economies.

Yet China was (and remains) an autocratic state, and continues to pay scant regard to human rights – as was clearly demonstrated by the massacre of hundreds of democratic protesters in Beijing's Tiananmen Square in 1989. When

---

[109] *Why the West Rules for Now* by Ian Morris, Profile Books.

Western governments attempted to make trade contingent upon an improvement in the country's attitude towards human rights, China responded angrily, claiming that human rights monitoring violated its sovereignty. Shamefully sacrificing human rights considerations for economic interest, Western governments rapidly capitulated, although the arms embargo imposed on China in the wake of the massacre remains in place. Economic power was becoming increasingly important.

The Resurgence of Islam

The post-Cold War era also saw a religious revival – split between Orthodox Christianity and Islam – in the former communist states, and in Asia, where China experienced a huge increase in the number of converts to Christianity. The Islamic world, however, perhaps seeing the relative decline in Western power and prestige as a sign of moral decay, became increasingly hostile to the West. The Cold War between two superpowers was replaced by a civilisational Cold War between Islam and the West. Samuel Huntington, in his seminal work, *The Clash of Civilizations*, asserted that this 'Islamic Resurgence' was at least as relevant as the Protestant Reformation and the revolutions in France, America and Russia. Several Islamic states, through their strategic locations, large populations and oil resources, became increasingly influential in world affairs. Within these, Islamic movements rejecting Western secularism, decadence and immorality began to dominate the opposition to their autocratic governments.

Huge population growth in Islamic countries, increasing migration to cities and several years of drought led to growing unemployment, hunger and social unrest. Extremists managed to capitalise on this anger. The first decade of the 21st century saw an increase in terrorist attacks perpetrated by Muslim extremists convinced that it was the duty of all Muslims to wage war against non-believers. These included a devastating attack on the World Trade Centre in New York on September 11th 2001, and bombings in Bali (2002), Madrid (2004) and London (2005).

America responded to the attack on the World Trade Centre by initiating a global 'war on terror', invading Afghanistan in 2001 and Iraq in 2003. It was supported by the UK and other western European powers. Despite ridding the world of Saddam Hussein and his odious sons who had raped, tortured, poisoned and butchered their fellow country men, and despite temporarily denting the fortunes of al-Qaeda, both wars were heavily, and justly, criticised for inadequate planning and the huge human and financial costs they entailed. In Iraq alone, over 100,000 people died, and the cost of these wars has been estimated at over a trillion US dollars. Foreign troops left Iraq only in 2011 and Afghanistan only in 2014 having totally failed to install any semblance of order.

The region was thrown into further chaos in 2010 by the 'Arab Spring' – a movement that began in Tunisia in protest against the region's incompetent, corrupt and morally bankrupt elites. Widespread discontent over unemployment and low living standards were major contributing factors. A sectarian bloodbath spread across the region in which a number of Arab despots were removed from power.

In Syria, a brutal response to unrest by the ruling party in 2011 led to a civil war in which over 500,000 (including 55,000 children) died. Over five million Syrians fled their country and an even greater number was displaced internally. The country was effectively, and tragically, destroyed. Into this vacuum stepped a jihadist regime so brutal that it made past efforts at genocide look like child's play: ISIS. While as of

2019, the Caliphate that ISIS attempted to create has officially been pulverised, the world has undoubtedly not heard the last from its brainwashed adherents.

Millions of Syrians were forced to flee the country, and many of them sought refuge in Europe via several well-known smuggling routes. Europe's response was to do everything in its power to deter them from coming. Those that did manage to survive the crossing of the Mediterranean were detained in squalid, disease-ridden camps for months on end.

WHAT'S NEXT?

In the 20th century we climbed the highest mountains, visited the extremes of the earth, and even landed a machine on another planet. What we have achieved as a species is quite spectacular. In many ways, we currently live in the best of times: we have unlimited and cheap energy at our disposal and access to medicine unparalleled in human history; we can visit any part of the planet within 24 hours, and falling costs of computing and communications have contributed to bringing down barriers of every kind. In theory, we should be at our cultural zenith.

Paradoxically, however, the last century also witnessed the worst wars in history, and even with our best minds we are still unable to free the vast majority of the world's population from the 'poverty trap'. Despite so many advances in science, education and communications, modern-day slavery – in the form of human trafficking – continues to be a blight upon the world, and is becoming one of the fastest-growing criminal activities. Millions of people around the world remain in forced labour and children are regularly being trafficked for commercial gain.[110] Our endless hankering after material gain and possessions has led to an explosion of debt, and to a crisis in our financial system. We are no closer to the perfect political system than the ancient Greeks were.

The resurgence of Islamic militancy threatens the very basis upon which modern Western society was built: free thought, democracy and the rule of law. It also threatens the supply

---

[110] http://www.unglobalcompact.org

of oil, much of which lies in the Islamic countries of Saudi Arabia, Iran, Iraq and Kuwait. If this supply is threatened, the West and its trading partners will suffer the consequences, and the result will be further instability and conflict.

Yet there is a much larger threat to global prosperity and world peace than a shaky economy or an unstable oil supply, as serious as they are. This threat is climate change. Despite clear evidence of the consequences of doing so, we pollute the vulnerable climate in which we live, inadvertently destroying the environmental resources upon which we, as a species, depend. In an endless drive for profit, we destroy the forests which are needed to produce oxygen and reduce carbon dioxide – a large contributor to the heating of our planet – and through our addiction to hydrocarbons, we continue to pollute the air we breathe and the water we drink.

Many previous societies have collapsed from overexploitation of resources. This is exactly what we are doing now, but on a global scale. We know the problems we are storing up for ourselves, but our constant short-termism and lack of political will to make unpopular decisions mean that we do nothing about it. We live in a state of denial.

We may be immensely adaptable as a species, but with the world's population now at over seven billion and growing, at some point demand for vital resources such as water may well exceed supply. Unless we begin to think ahead, and do something to preserve our valuable resources, we will end up fighting over them, and then the future is very likely to consist of intolerance, warfare, starvation and genocide, as it has done in the past.

FURTHER INFORMATION

Comments
With such a broad subject to cover, it is clearly difficult to please everybody. Feedback, comments and/or corrections are gratefully accepted by the author. Please send these to info@lascelleshistory.com

Timeline
A timeline of world history wall map is available for purchase at www.lascelleshistory.com.

Twitter
The author's twitter handle is @historymeister

Also by Christopher Lascelles

PONTIFEX MAXIMUS
A Short History of the Popes

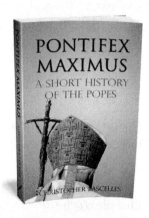

"A brilliant book on a number of different levels. Lascelles has an engaging prose style and an amazing eye for detail and apposite anecdote. Surely only purblind Catholic zelanti will object to this outstanding analysis."
Frank McLynn, author of Genghis Khan, Napoleon and 1066

"Lascelles has achieved the seemingly impossible: a concise and highly readable history of Catholic popes that manages to be extremely entertaining and informative at the same time."
Gerald Posner, author of God's Bankers

"Pontifex Maximus is a subtle and convincing explanation of how the successors of an impoverished fisherman from Galilee became globally powerful monarchs – all without getting lost in the bewildering historical weeds. Lascelles writes with both verve and humor. Once started it's hard to put down."
Lars Brownworth, author of The Normans

"Lascelles has taken an overwhelming subject, and not been overwhelmed by it in any way. A highly enjoyable read."
Paul Strathern, author of The Medici

For many people, the popes are an irrelevance: if they consider them at all, it may be as harmless old men who preach obscure sermons in Latin. But the history of the popes is far from bland. On the contrary, it is occasionally so bizarre as to stretch credulity. Popes have led papal armies, fled in disguise, fathered children (including future popes), and authorised torture. They have been captured, assaulted and murdered. While many have been respected, others have been hated to such a degree that their funeral processions have been disrupted and statues of them torn down after their deaths. Many have been the enemies of freedom and progress – divisive rather than unifying figures.

In a fascinating and engaging read, Christopher Lascelles examines the history of the popes through the ages, laying bare the extent to which many of them fell so very short of the Christian ideals they supposedly represented. He explains how it was that, professing to follow a man who said 'My kingdom is not of this world' and 'Lay not up for yourselves treasures upon earth', they nevertheless became the heads of a rich state that owned more land in Europe than any king, relying on foreign military aid to keep power; and how pride, greed and corruption became commonplace in an institution founded on love, faith and forgiveness.

This book is aimed at the general reader who is short on time and seeks an accessible overview unencumbered by ecclesiastical jargon and scholarly controversies.

INDEX

Page numbers including an **m** indicate reference to a map. Those including an **n** mean that the information is within the notes only.

Made in the USA
Las Vegas, NV
05 April 2021

20858121R00154